BENT POLES & TIGHT LINES
CHARLES E. SALTER

PEACHTREE PUBLISHERS LIMITED
Atlanta, Georgia

Published by
PEACHTREE PUBLISHERS LIMITED
494 Armour Circle, N. E., Atlanta, Georgia 30324

Copyright © 1982 Charles E. Salter

All rights reserved. No part of this book may be reproduced in any form or by any means without the prior written permission of the Publisher, excepting brief quotes used in connection with reviews, written specifically for inclusion in a magazine or newspaper.

Manufactured in the United States of America.

Cover design by Norm Kohn.

First edition

Library of Congress Catalog Number 82-081839
ISBN: 0-931948-33-9

To my father, the late
J. D. Salter,
my best friend, a gifted teacher,
and a great angler.

Contents

Foreword by Tom Mann   viii

I BLUEGILL
The No. 1 Pan Fish	3
On Reservoir Shores	8
A Fish for All Seasons	11
Light Tackle, Big Thrills	15
Babe Ruth of Bream Anglers	19
Spinning Lures Bring Action	23
A Little Corner of Heaven on Earth	25
Outwit 'Em With a Glow	27

II LARGEMOUTH BASS
Greatest Freshwater Game Fish	33
"Get the Net, Honey"	40
Teenager Lands Two "Hawgs"	44
Phillip's World-Record Catch	47
A Fountain of Youth	49
Spoon-Jigging in Winter	52
Confidence Is the Best Lure	57
Country Boy's Instinct	60
A Silent Lunker-Hunter	67
Top-Water Bassin' Evangelist	73
Big Plugs, Big Fish	79

III TROUT
Casting Close to Home	83
An Unforgettable Battle	86
The Secret—Natural Movement	89
Natives Offer a Challenge	91
Trophies Galore	93
Dedication Required	96
An Inexpensive Catch	99
Double Strikes	101
The Fever Is Contagious	103

IV	CRAPPIE	
	Mr. and Mrs. Papermouth	107
	A Crappie Champion	109
	Smiling Minnows Are Best	112
	Deadly Little Jigs	115
	Trolling, Casting, and Dipping	117
	Trophy Almost Became a Meal	125
V	REDBREAST	
	Royalty of River Pan Fish	129
VI	STRIPED BASS	
	Streamlined Champs	139
	"A Whole New Ball Game"	143
	"Hey, Where Are We Going?"	146
	Stripers Love Bluegills	149
	New Reel Passes Test	152
	Schooling Stripers—A Thrill a Minute	154
	Big Ones Feed at Night	156
	Tracking the Stripers	158
	Striper Honeymoon	161
	Trolling for Trophies	164
	Spooning in Winter	165
VII	WHITE BASS	
	Give Them a High Grade	169
	Did a World Record Shrink?	172
	Hitting the Bullseye	175
	Pass the Minnows, Please	177
	April Fever for White Bass	179
VIII	WALLEYE	
	Fair Fighter, Delicious Dinner	185
IX	SHELLCRACKER	
	Real Pole-Benders	193
X	JACKFISH	
	Ol' Chain Sides—A Real Battler	199

XI	CATFISH	
	You'll Live Longer	209
	A Lazy Man's Job	214
	Watch Your Line "Breathe"	217
XII	BOWFIN	
	His Name Is Mud	223
	Record-Breaking Living Fossil	225
	An Unwanted Monster	227
XIII	DABBLING—"JIGGER-FISHING"	
	For Explosive Strikes	231
XIV	FISH TALES—SOME TALL, SOME TRUE	
	Fudgey Finds the Biguns	239
	Leroy—A Fighter and Lover	243
	Bulger—An Angling Legend	247
	Hey! Stop That Bird!	250
XV	ILLUSTRATIONS	
	Improved Clinch Knot	255
	Palomar Knot	257
	Carolina Rig	259
	Texas Rig	261

Foreword

It would take most fishermen a lifetime to learn everything Charles Salter has put in *Bent Poles and Tight Lines*. He has been giving his wisdom away in his column in *The Atlanta Journal* since 1969—here are the most valuable tips. If a man will read everything that Charlie writes about fishing, he will be ten times the fisherman.

I have been knowing Charles Salter a long time. You can bank on what he writes about fishing—it's the truth. Charlie and I have caught fantastic fish together and we have lost fantastic fish together. He is one of the most dedicated anglers I have ever met. But, ol' Charlie doesn't feel like he's got to hang them on the wall or show them off. He has baked more lunkers than most fishermen will ever catch. He doesn't want a trophy or a cash prize—he wants a challenge.

Charlie is not so smart. He's like Br'er Fox—he just can't think any slower. Sometimes I call him Br'er Charlie. Years ago his father told him, "You'll never learn it all." Charlie has never stopped learning. We have sat and studied fish in aquariums for hours, eyeball to eyeball with bass, bream, and crappie. We have watched how they respond to different lures—tried to understand their behavior. Charlie has experimented with more types of fishing lures over the years than anybody else I know.

I wouldn't say he's a purist, but Charlie has a great appreciation of technique. Now, he's caught two big tarpon in

Florida on consecutive days—each one about 6 feet long, weighing about 125 pounds. But, he'll tell you his biggest thrill in fishing was catching an 8-pound largemouth bass on a 6-pound line with an ultra light spinning reel and a rod with the action of a willow branch. He knows the charge of hooking a bluegill or shellcracker on a fly rod. He knows that's the ultimate in angling.

Charlie doesn't just talk to pros. During all of those years of writing the outdoor column, he has had the chance to pick the brains of the local experts. He has fished with everybody, but his regular fishing buddies include a truck driver, an auto mechanic, a bus driver, and a retired postmaster. He says he had a great time fishing with a member of the SWAT Squad, whom he described as being "a gentle, soft-spoken guy with incredible aim."

Charlie and I are going bass fishing again soon. We have caught bass on jelly worms, Little Georges, and on experimental bait you wouldn't believe. We'll go back to Lake Eufaula, where we're still trying to catch Ol' Ned, that humongous bass that would break all records. (Charlie calls her Ol' Nelly, because the females are bigger.) We have each seen the other hook that lunker and lose him.

But, a successful fishing trip is happiness—it's how you feel on the lake. You can't measure it by what you catch. If you can just sit back and relax and see the snakes lying on the limbs and watch the wildlife all around you, it's got to be good for you. Get Charlie to go fishing with you if you can. If you can't, just take *Bent Poles and Tight Lines* along with you, and you'll feel like he's in the other end of the boat.

Tom Mann
Eufaula, Alabama

The author's son, Chuck Salter, was proud of this mixed string of bluegills and largemouth bass that he caught several years ago in a farm pond.

I
Bluegill

Bobby Reese, operator of a fishing tackle store in Riverdale, Ga., holds one of the many big bluegills that he and the author caught in a farm pond while casting and also trolling little curly-tailed yellow jigs. The jigs, which Reese designed, also drew strikes from yearling largemouth bass.

The No. 1 Pan Fish

My favorite pan fish and one of the most popular in the entire South is the bluegill, a truly great fighter that is a member of the sunfish family.

Short and deep-bodied, with a small head and mouth, the bluegill has a black gill flap, a dark blotch on the back part of its dorsal fin, and seven or eight dark vertical bars on its sides.

Colors of these pan fish vary in the farm ponds, rivers, and reservoirs. I have caught many bluegills that had dark blue sides, while others had more of a yellowish hue, and some appear closer to olive green in shade.

The old-timers develop so much body depth that they look humpbacked, and their heads flatten out as if they had collided with a stump while trying to outswim a competitor for an insect.

During the spring when water temperatures rise to 70 to 75 degrees, bluegills move close to the shallow banks and the upper ends of ponds and reservoir coves to build saucer-shaped nests. A single female may deposit up to twenty-five to thirty thousand or more eggs.

The odor of bluegills' nests reminds some fishermen of over-ripe watermelons, while others describe it as a sweet, musty scent. Once a nesting area is located, a fisherman can sit on the bank or anchor his johnboat within cane pole or casting distance and catch huge numbers of these pan fish by baiting No. 8 or No. 6 hooks with such baits as crickets, red wigglers, small Louisiana pinks, barnyard wigglers, or grasshoppers.

In the summer when the bluegills are in deeper water, golden grubs and catalpa worms are excellent baits.

Here in the Deep South, we call the bluegill a "bream," and we must explain to visitors from the North that bream rhymes with "rim," not "cream."

Bream were the first fish that my two daughters, Suzanne and Laura, and my son, Chuck, ever caught, and my children began to understand what I meant when I confessed to having a serious case of "fishing fever."

When Chuck was five years old, we rode from our Atlanta home to central Georgia to fish in a farm pond, stopping first at a country store to buy bait. Chuck was disappointed that there weren't any crickets available, but I assured him that bream also were crazy about red wigglers.

A few minutes later we were sitting on the pond's bank under a big oak tree. Chuck frowned and observed, "That hook isn't very big."

I explained, "A bream has a small mouth, so we can catch them better with this No. 8 hook. We'll pinch one piece of this lead, called split shot, about six inches above the hook, and that'll make the worm sink to the bottom."

He asked, "Why did you put that red and white thing on the line?"

I said, "That's a float or bobber. It floats on top of the water, and when a bream nibbles on the worm, we can see the float move off or go under the water. Then we know a fish has got the worm in his mouth, and we set the hook."

"Do you think we're gonna catch many fish?" he asked.

I replied, "I hope so. Some days they bite, and some days they don't."

My blue-eyed blond son was filled with enthusiasm and optimism on this, his first, fishing trip. He wanted so much to catch some fish and have a big story to tell his mother and sisters. He couldn't imagine how much I wanted him to catch some bream.

As we got our fishing tackle ready, a frog jumped into the water nearby, and several startled bream darted toward the safety of deeper spots, and a largemouth bass made a splash as it struck a minnow close to the shore.

I made a cast with Chuck's new closed-face reel, and we settled back with great expectations and he watched his "cork." It may be a float or bobber made of plastic or wood, but here in Georgia we call it a cork.

In a moment the cork twitched and began moving across the surface. Chuck jerked the fiberglass 5½-foot rod up and began rapidly turning the reel's handle. The limber rod bent, and my son felt a thrill that he never had known.

"I've got him," he said. "I've got him."

The bream turned at a right angle, tugging and pulling with every ounce of power it could muster. My proud son pulled the little fighter to the bank and beamed as if he had just broken a fishing record.

Soon he was back on his feet struggling with another bluegill, this one a bit heavier. "How does that one feel, Chuck?" I asked.

Grinning from ear to ear and clutching the reel close to his chest, he said, "This is a mean one, Daddy. He's really pulling hard."

A few minutes later my cork began a journey across the surface to deeper water, and I handed my cane pole to Chuck. At first the pole seemed too long for him to handle, but he gripped it tightly in both hands as the battling bluegill dashed to the right and left.

This fish soon joined his cousins on our stringer, and we stayed in that same spot until Chuck had caught 21 bluegills, a pretty fair mess of fish for any angler.

As we were putting our fishing tackle into the car and preparing to return home, Chuck looked once more at the lovely pond and asked, "Daddy, when can we go fishing again? I like to catch bream. They're fun."

A number of fishing trips later, when Chuck was 13, we fished in the same pond with red wigglers in April. The pond owner, a farmer, had encouraged us by observing, "Believe if you hold your mouth right, you'll catch a mess of bream."

I wondered if a cool spell so early in the spring had affected fish appetites, and we noticed the pond was rather muddy from showers of the previous day. Deciding not to use the johnboat, we walked along the bank to watch for ripples and fish-feeding activity.

Two weeks earlier I had caught a few bream and some bass with a yellow spinning lure and silver blade, but this day only one small bass hit. A popping bug on my fly rod produced no strikes.

We sat on the bank and baited our small hooks with red wigglers and made long casts, then began watching the red-and-white corks. Our baits seemed to be too safe for comfort. Nothing touched them. It was time for a switch in strategy.

I remembered a seemingly unrelated line from a burlesque scene in an old movie. A nearly over-the-hill dancer told a pretty young newcomer backstage, "Honey, you've got to keep it moving."

Maybe this would work in bream fishing, too. Move the bait so the fish will notice it. I advised Chuck, "Move your bait a little bit across the bottom, and see what happens."

I used the same tactic, and my cork jumped as if it had hiccups, and it slowly was pulling away. I set the hook in the mouth of a beautiful, hand-size bluegill which fought like the pond champion.

Chuck made a long cast into the same shallow area, let his bait sink to the bottom, then raised the rod tip several inches, dragging the worm. He paused, and the cork slowly moved off.

Chuck laughed, set the hook, and said, "Got him."

In that muddy water the bluegills seemed only half-interested, nibbling and backing away, then taking another bite. Concentration and patience were required in order to set the hook at the right time. I confess that each of us got a bit overanxious and missed two or three fish.

Several yearling bass also hit the lively red wigglers in the three-foot-deep water, and we landed two handsome shellcrackers that had been building or guarding nests.

Before the sun sank out of sight behind a big stand of pine trees, Chuck and I had put on our stringer a fine mess of bluegills, shellcrackers, and two bass.

The success of the day, however, wasn't measured in numbers or pounds of fish.

We were pals—a father and his son enjoying the great outdoors on a gorgeous spring day, laughing and talking miles from the tension and hustle and bustle of the city.

When Chuck pulled out a bluegill wider than his hand and proudly held up the fish to admire it, I remembered how a tall, skinny blond boy in Waycross, Georgia, years earlier got fishing lessons from his father.

That blond fellow, now balding and weighing twice as much, still regarded his fishing teacher as the best pal he ever had. I regret that the gentle and good man did not live to see his grandson become a teenager and discover the great joys of fishing.

On Reservoir Shores

An Atlanta friend told me that every spring and summer he catches large numbers of bluegills in 38,000-acre Lake Sidney Lanier.

He fishes with a closed-face spinner, baits his little hooks with red wigglers or crickets, and slowly eases along the shore in his boat with the aid of an electric motor.

"Lanier has got a lot of bream," he said. "And you'd be surprised at the size of some of 'em."

His experience reminded me of the day in late June a few years ago when Perry Roberts and I fished for bream on Lake Hartwell, a 55,950-acre lake in Georgia and South Carolina. Since impoundment in 1962, Hartwell has been known for fine largemouth bass, white bass, and crappie fishing, and in recent years striped bass and hybrid bass have gained in popularity, but relatively few people fish for bream there.

Early in May, Perry and another man had boated their limits of bream in Hartwell. Later in May he, his wife, and a neighbor strung 150 Hartwell bream.

On a windy, surprisingly cool morning under gray clouds, Perry and I launched my bass boat in Hartwell and headed for a cove that he had found to be productive on an earlier trip. I turned on the bow-mounted electric motor and we moved slowly near the bank.

Both of us used 12-foot, telescopic fiberglass poles, 10-pound monofilament line, one split shot, and a little oblong cork secured 18 inches above a No. 8 hook baited with a cricket. We pitched the crickets close to grass, brush, and logs, let the bait stay a few seconds, and then put it in another spot.

My partner's first bite was from a bream that yanked the cork out of sight, and I boated a bluegill that pulled the cork in a sneaky fashion only inches beneath the surface.

In the upper end of a cove, we spotted freshly fanned beds soon after picking up the watermelon-like scent of bluegill nests.

Zipping back and forth in the water, my line fairly sang as a rugged bluegill put a respectable bow in my fishing pole. Then my partner grunted, "Uhhh, uhhh . . . it's a good one."

By five o'clock in the afternoon we had put 130 bream in the boat and released 30 of them, keeping our legal limit for the day.

"Did you ever think you could have a ball like this, pulling bream out of Lake Hartwell?" Perry asked. "I told you this lake is running over with bream. They're in these coves. People just don't fish for them like they do for crappie and bass. You'll have to look a long way before you find a fish that fights better, ounce for ounce, than this bluegill."

Ike Williams was fishing with a pink worm almost 20 feet deep when this handsome bluegill decided it was lunchtime.

A Fish for All Seasons

Ike Williams lives on a lake a few miles north of Atlanta, and he likes to go fishing in his spare time the year-round. I knew that he enjoyed considerable success catching bream in the spring and summer, but I was surprised to learn that he hooks them by the dozens in the autumn and manages to put a few bluegills in the boat even in December.

On a bluebird day in mid-October, he invited me to fish with him in his 12-foot aluminum boat on the clear lake with a steep, beautiful shore that reminded me of a mountain lake. The air was slightly chilly, the cool wind cut a ripple across the water's surface, and we heard birds sing occasionally in the oaks, dogwoods, maples, poplars, and sweetgums. Fat squirrels were scurrying around on the bank gathering food for the winter. If the birds and squirrels were active, perhaps the fish would be ready to eat, too.

In the autumn, I'm usually casting plugs for largemouth bass and schooling white bass or using little jigs to fool crappie in reservoirs.

Ike figured this would be a fine day to catch bream on crickets. Most fishermen probably still think bream fishing is just done in warm weather. The crickets are nearly as effective bait in the autumn; you just have to fish deeper.

My friend prefers to fish with a long, very limber fiberglass pole, No. 8 gold hook, and a highly visible bobber—red or chartreuse—three feet or more above his bait.

"When that cork's doing something unnatural, something it's not supposed to do," he said, "set the hook. The bream's got the cricket in his mouth."

We moved quietly in the johnboat parallel to the bank, gently dropping our crickets into water ranging from three to almost twenty feet in depth. We adjusted the corks so that the bait sometimes was only three feet beneath the surface.

Ike and I caught eight bream that hit at depths of three to six feet. When action became slow, we lowered our baits as deep as nine feet.

Cork-watching is one of those wonderful tranquilizers that can't be bought across a counter in a drugstore. Write yourself a prescription for joy and relaxation, and your days on earth surely will be more in number.

Ike was right about those sly bluegills in the autumn. Several times they pulled the bobber under and darted away, cricket and hook in mouth. But, sometimes they just made the cork tremble so slightly that a drowsy angler might think it was merely wave action.

"On a long fiberglass pole like this," said Ike, "you can enjoy every ounce of that bream. It might even convert some of those bass fishermen."

This remark was made by a fellow who has caught numerous big black bass, including a 12 lb. 8 oz. beauty hanging on his wall.

The surface temperature of the water was 64 degrees, and the bream were quite scattered. After the water chills to the high 50s, the bream will congregate at depths of 10 to 20 feet.

"I'll be catching bream weighing ¾ of a pound to 1 pound or better in late October and throughout November," Ike said. "But, then I'll be fishing on the bottom in deep water with Louisiana pinks."

By late afternoon we had dropped about 25 large bluegills into Ike's wire basket and released two dozen little fish. Ike felt we would have caught many more if a sudden cool spell, accompanied by wind, hadn't arrived the previous night. On the patio of his house, the mercury had dipped to a low of 42 degrees, making the few remaining tomatoes on the vines stop smiling.

Ike's success with bream cannot be attributed to luck. He searches for bluegills with the diligence and patience of a pointer looking for a covey of quail. I'll bet that a freight car could hardly hold all of the bluegills and shellcrackers that Ike has put in his aluminum johnboat in the past 30 years.

* * *

Several more times that autumn I had the privilege of fishing with Ike for bream in that lake. On December 1, I pulled a 1 lb. 2 oz. bluegill out of 20 feet of cold water.

Some of our biggest bream were caught on a chilly, drizzly Saturday in November when the water was 58 degrees. He had called and said, "Let's try 'em this afternoon. Bring your rainsuit. I think they'll bite around four o'clock and keep it up until nearly dark."

The rain had turned to a cool mist when we began baiting hooks with Louisiana pinks after anchoring the johnboat so we could cast the worms into water 15 to 20 feet deep. Ike invited five beautiful bluegills to dinner, and we moved to another hole where I began playing catch-up.

In the next two hours we added 19 great-grandmama and great-grandpapa bream to the stringer. Our catch totaled 24 of the finest looking bluegills I've ever seen. More than half of them weighed a pound each. We didn't even count the small bream we had released.

We had to use sliding sinkers and two split shot to cast far enough to reach the deep-water bream from the spot where we anchored. Some of the bream grabbed the worms, yanking the corks under on short runs; others nibbled and made the corks dance on the surface.

"They've been taking it better than this," said Ike. "Other afternoons they'd bite and go, and if you didn't grab the rod and reel, they'd pull it out of the boat. It can get kind of interesting when you get two bites at the same time."

This happened to me half an hour before sunset, and I handed my Zebco 33 closed-face reel and rod to Ike, while I picked up the little Zebco 144, a combination spinning and spin-cast reel, and we boated two fully grown bluegills. It's great fun to feel a bream, bigger than your hand, tugging and running against a reel's light drag and bending a graphite-and-fiberglass ultra-light rod into an unbelievably sharp bow.

I've felt for years that if a bluegill reached a weight of eight or ten pounds, a fisherman would need saltwater tackle to land him.

Perhaps I should have taken my tape recorder to that lake to pick up the beautiful, musical sound of a reel's drag screaming or a bluegill splashing at the side of the boat. On a dreary, cold, gray day in January or February in Atlanta, I could listen to lovely sounds and remember the marvelous feeling of fighting a mean, stubborn bream.

Light Tackle, Big Thrills

Bill Barber of Decatur, Georgia, is one of the South's greatest bluegill fishermen. He catches these pan fish kings and queens of farm ponds ten or eleven months out of the year, fishing from the banks or in a johnboat with an electric trolling motor.

To fully appreciate every ounce of the bream's fighting qualities, says Bill, you've got to use light and ultra-light tackle.

He fishes with a Zebco 33 closed-face reel, a Mitchell spinning reel, a Zebco 144 combination spinning and spin-cast reel—mounted under the rod and with a trip lever for line release on a cast—and an old, closed-face reel that is secured under a seven-foot rod. The rod was made by Bill and has the extremely light action of a fly rod.

Bill ties a small knot with fishing line on his monofilament line so that, as the baited hook sinks in the water, the cork will rise on the line and stop at the knot for a predetermined fishing depth. This rig works fine when he fishes a cricket two to four feet deep, and it also is suitable when he wants to offer a live worm on the bottom in shallow water.

"When I am looking for bream, I can fish this rod and move the bait slowly on the bottom until I drag it up to them," he said. "The bream may smell the bait, or they may see it moving."

To be a successful fisherman, you have to realize it quickly when you are in unproductive water—anglers who leave their bait in one spot too long waste a lot of time. Even while fishing a cricket under a cork, it pays to let it lie in one place only a short time before moving it a bit to attract attention.

Bill likes a gold No. 8 hook, figuring it may have appeal when reflecting the light; also, when the hook becomes hung on a snag or stump, he can exert pressure and force it to bend and come free without snapping his line—usually.

He showed me a fly-fishing lure an acquaintance designed—a black sponge body with white legs—that is very effective for bream when fished under a water-filled plastic bobber. A split shot pinched on the line permits him to make longer casts. This bait should be quite deadly in the spring, when bream are nesting in shallow water.

Another artificial lure that Bill uses is a very short, skinny black plastic worm with two tiny hooks.

"That little hook helps you catch a bream that bites the worm's tail instead of the head," he said. "Sometimes a yearling bass will strike it too."

Sometimes, he fishes a tight line without a cork, a method that requires attentive line-watching. A bluegill's shy, sneaky bite might be indicated by nothing more than a little "blink" on the six-pound test line.

A catalpa worm is one of the best bream baits, though an awfully messy critter. Bill sometimes makes two baits out of one worm.

During the late autumn and winter when the water is cold and the bream are lying in deeper holes, Bill bundles up in heavy clothing and offers them a different bait.

"That is the time to bait your hook with golden grubs or the mighty mealy [a meal worm]," he said. "I sometimes catch bigger bream in the winter than in the summer.

"You can use four-, six-, or eight-pound test line on an ultra-light spinning reel. Sometimes I use eight-pound line, but my friend Jack McGee uses four-pound line. You see, I've got an eight-pound snatch when I set the hook."

Either a No. 6 or No. 8 hook is satisfactory, and you can use two or three golden grubs at a time to make the menu more attractive. Jack uses a sliding sinker and fishes on the bottom without a cork. Bill uses a swivel to stop the lead 14 inches above the hook.

"They don't bite quite as fast when the water is cool," he said. "You cast out there in deep water—8 to 15 feet deep—and wait for a bite. If nothing touches your bait, move it a little bit, maybe two turns of the reel's handle. Sometimes that'll attract the bream.

"A smaller bait than the popular red wiggler, the golden grub has little or no action in the water, but its color and size are appealing to bream, and I think there might be an odor they notice, too," Bill observed.

Studies by biologists in a Midwestern state several years ago showed that a bream consumes food totaling over three hundred percent of its body weight between May and October, but in other months when the water is quite cold, the fish's food requirements amount to only 13 percent of its body weight.

Bill said that the mighty mealy, "a super worm for bream fishing," is about two times as long as its ½-inch cousin, the golden grub. One of his friends caught more than four hundred bluegills in several trips to farm ponds and explained he gave the little worm even more appeal by putting one spoonful of Bait Mate oil in each cup of bait.

"This gives them a kind of sheen or luster that the bream just can't turn down," Jack McGee told Bill and me. "I know a fellow who put the oil on a mighty mealy and caught a 26-inch brown trout in a north Georgia stream."

Bill said, "I believe the mighty mealy was developed in California. They must have been feeding this worm something special to jazz up its size."

* * *

While Bill was operating a bait shop a number of years in Atlanta, I had the opportunity to join in bull sessions about fishing with two of his old bream-hooking buddies, Jack McGee and Buddy Born.

One day in October, Jack and Buddy baited hooks with golden grubs and fished four hours in a five-acre pond near Atlanta, and they boated 54 bluegills that averaged ½ pound, the biggest going 1 lb. 2 oz. They fished on the bottom in 9 to 14 feet of water.

"I like to catch bream on ultra-light tackle," said Jack. "I think it is tops in fishing. The line is four-pound-test monofilament, the reel is an ultra-light spinner, and the rod is 6½ feet long and weighs only 2½ ounces. There's just no thrill like it in fishing."

Like his friend Bill Barber, he prefers the tight-line method without a cork.

"I walk the bait," Jack explained. "I do it with the reel handle, not the rod. You just slowly turn the handle and make the bait drag across the bottom of a lake. You let it go a little way and then stop it, and if a bream doesn't take it, you move it again. You move it twice and they'll nail it. It irritates them."

Babe Ruth of Bream Anglers

In a period of just three years, Buddy Born pulled out of farm ponds 300 bluegills that each weighed one pound or more. I believe that must be the fishing equivalent of a baseball player knocking 60 home runs in each of three consecutive seasons.

A native of Atlanta, Buddy developed an interest in fishing when he was 14 years old, dug red wigglers out of a hog pen behind an old stockyard, and caught bream and small catfish in Nancy Creek. Later he and a friend built a johnboat, baited hooks with minnows, and cut bait and fished trotlines in the Chattahoochee River, catching catfish in the 1½- to 4-pound class.

Almost 20 years ago he got hooked on bream fishing with ultra-light spinning reels and four-pound-test line in small ponds, and he and his friend Jack McGee put hand-size bluegills on their stringers ten months out of the year. If bream fishing tournaments were held, these two fellows probably would alternate finishing first and second in most of the events.

"I caught fish in shallow water in a pond when the water was cold," Buddy said. "At one time the water was 44 degrees. Someone said they wouldn't bite. The next morning he asked what I had used for bait. I told him. He said he didn't think they'd bite. I caught eight or nine bream that weighed close to a pound each."

His largest bream that day weighed 1 lb. 6 oz., and the wind nearly blew him off the pond.

Buddy has fished with red wigglers, crickets, and catalpa worms, but he catches more bluegills and larger fish on the mighty mealy worms.

"I put two on a hook and use a ⅛-ounce-slip sinker, plus a BB lead, and put the BB 12 inches above the hook. I don't use a cork.

"I fish the mighty mealy on the bottom. Sometimes you can't feel it when the bream bites. You have to watch the line. Sometimes the big ones just sit there and hold it or swallow it. You have to watch the line, and when it moves, tighten the line and set the hook."

A bream sometimes takes the bait so gently that a person using heavier fishing tackle wouldn't know he'd had a bite.

Buddy fishes with an ultra-light, 6½-foot rod and a small spinning reel and No. 8 hook, and an electric motor pushes the aluminum johnboat to his honey holes on the ponds.

I was curious about the length of the bluegill feeding period in a pond.

"I have fished in a pond from seven o'clock in the morning until four-thirty or five o'clock in the evening, and they were still biting when I left," he said. "I go fishing whenever I get a chance. Some times I don't catch as many as I do others. If it's beautiful, I love to be out there."

His biggest bream ever was a 1 lb. 9 oz. trophy that he hooked in a pond a few miles east of Atlanta.

In the winter he hooks many bluegills in six or seven feet of water, but in the spring and early summer when they are spawning, he pulls them out of water one to three feet deep close to the banks and in upper ends of ponds. He prefers to fish water with a bottom that is "a little bit snaggy."

During the hottest part of the summer, Buddy has good luck with catalpa worms and crickets, but 90 percent of his bream fishing is done with mighty mealies on the bottom.

Buddy gives the bluegill a grade of A-plus as a fighter.

"Well, I'd have to argue with the bass fishermen," he said, laughing. "A bream will fight longer than a bass. If a bream weighed five or six pounds, I don't believe you could hold him. I hung that 1 lb. 9 oz. bream, and he went around so hard he got plumb out of the water and went onto the edge of the bank. There wasn't a whole lot I could do. He was pulling on that rod and running so hard. I hemmed him up. A shellcracker will fight faster than a bluegill—at the beginning he will snatch the rod out of the boat. But, in a minute he slows down.

"One day in Bill's bait shop, I was kidding Jack McGee about fishing with sewing thread—four-pound line. A bumblebee could collide with the line and break it," I said, ribbing him.

"No, I don't lose many fish," he said, grinning. "Every now and then one runs around a snag. I was fishing with a minnow one day on four-pound line and caught a ten-pound bass."

He has caught hundreds of bluegills and shellcrackers that qualified as "bigger than my hand"—truly trophy fish. But Jack would rather eat a bream than stare at it hanging on the wall. His largest bluegill weighed 2½ pounds, and his best shellcracker tipped the scales at 2 lb. 3 oz.

* * *

Another Georgia fisherman who favors golden grubs in bream fishing is W. R. Sloan of Macon, who in one year caught 600 bluegills that many anglers would have considered worthy of mounting on the wall. Sloan smiled and said, "One of these days I hope I can catch a two-pound bream, and then I'll have that one mounted."

He fishes with a featherweight, six-foot fly rod that his old friend Art Mickler designed especially for Sloan's style of angling on farm ponds.

"It's a very light fly rod," said Art. "I don't believe it would weigh over three ounces. A one-pound bluegill on that rod feels like a seven-pound largemouth bass on a baitcasting rod."

Sloan uses a small single-action fly reel, No. 5 line, and three or four feet of four-pound test monofilament leader. He doesn't use a split shot or float since it's a fly rod. He puts two or three golden grubs on a thin No. 6 Aberdeen hook and casts his bait.

"I like to fish from a small boat and cast the banks of a pond," said Sloan. "With this lightweight fly rod, I can roll those golden grubs under the bushes where the big bream are lying in the shade. You've got to watch the line closely. He'll pick up the golden grub and sometimes move just a little. Other times a bream will take it and run off."

He isn't concerned about the phase or position of the moon when he goes fishing. Numerous days in the spring and summer, he drives to a nearby pond after work and fishes until dark.

"The bream usually bite good late in the afternoon, and they really start hitting right at dark," he said. "My best catches have been during the spring, but I've also caught some big ones in the summer."

Sloan recalled a trip made to the Okefenokee Swamp many years ago. Fishing was a little slow, so he and his partner began wading and "cooning"—reaching under logs and into holes in stumps for fish.

"Suddenly a water moccasin popped up and looked my friend in the face," Sloan said. "The man spat in the moccasin's eyes and said, 'Go on, you rascal. I'm not fishing for you.' Then he slowly continued cooning under the logs and limbs."

Spinning Lures Bring Action

Small spinning lures sometimes are quite effective artificial baits in spring and summer when bream are moving and looking for food in the shallow water next to banks and in upper ends of farm ponds. If a johnboat isn't available, you can cover a considerable amount of water by casting from the shore.

Make several casts into the deeper water and bring back the small lure at a slow to medium retrieve, and a bream might mistake it for a minnow returning to safety and security of the weeds and grass next to the bank where he can hide from predators. Make a long cast to your left, then to your right, so that on the retrieve you are exposing the bait to fish in a sizable area in the shallows just off the bank.

The casts parallel to the bank likely will draw more strikes early in the morning and late in the afternoon when the surface is in the shade. In the summer when the warm sunshine heats up the shallows between nine o'clock and about five o'clock, the bream lie in deeper, slightly cooler water; therefore, the spinning lures should be cast into the open water and allowed to sink three to six feet before you begin the retrieve.

On a blistering afternoon in August, I stood on the dam of a three-acre pond and cast a spinning lure into the deep water, allowing it to sink nearly all the way to the bottom before I turned the reel's handle. I was rewarded with bites from half-a-dozen, hand-size bluegills that must have been lying at a depth of eight or nine feet.

When selecting spinning lures in a store for bream and shellcracker fishing, remember the pan fish have small mouths and the single or treble hooks must be a size that the fish can swallow.

I have had good luck fishing with the "O" and No. 1 size Mepps Spinners and Rooster Tails with the silver or the gold blades. The silver blade is recommended in clear water, while the gold-colored blade sometimes works better in stained water and on a cloudy day. There are days when a Mepps Spinner with squirrel-tail dressing on the back will catch more fish than the plain lure. A small spinning lure with a white or a pearl body may rank No. 1 on the fish biting charts today, but tomorrow you may discover the yellow bait is the best.

During the summer when the bluegills and shellcrackers are rather inactive in deeper water, you may change your luck by slowly trolling the spinning lures behind an electric motor on a johnboat.

Spinning lures should be fished on four- to six-pound test line with a light closed-face reel or an ultra-light spinning reel and an extremely limber rod five to six and one-half feet long. I prefer a very light spinning reel and a five- to six-foot rod that has the action of a little willow branch. For an even greater thrill in fighting the scrappy pan fish, put your light spinning reel on an eight-foot fiberglass fly rod. You will be able to make very long casts, and when the bluegill hits the lure, each rugged ounce can be even more fully appreciated.

A Little Corner of Heaven on Earth

The gorgeous, five-acre pond, bounded by a hardwood forest and a sprawling pasture where cows grazed in contentment, seemed a million miles from the hustling, bustling city. Cows look happy when they are eating grass, chewing their cuds, baby-sitting with calves, sleeping in the shade of oaks, and lapping water as they wade in a pond.

They are utterly unconcerned with traffic jams, crime, inflation, wages, ambition, status, politics, taxes, and skyrocketing electricity bills. Years ago in south Georgia, a guy assured me that if all the cows were chomping on grass, the fish in a pond also would be eating.

My fishing partner and I turned and looked toward the upper end of the pond after hearing splashes.

"Looks like an old bass has hemmed up some baby bream," he said, lighting his pipe. "Guess you could paraphrase the law of the jungle and say, 'In a pond, the big fish survive and the little ones perish.'"

Cows in a pasture never seem to be in a hurry, but a little fish in a pond must be alert and ready to floor-board his accelerator if he wants to live to see another sunrise.

Two turtles basking in the sunshine on a log slipped into the water as our johnboat slowly and quietly moved past them. A snake, his head barely poking above the surface, swam toward the bank, and I expected any second to see Old Mossy Jaws strike in an effort to swallow him.

My partner, fishing with a fly rod, removed the hook of his little green sponge bug from a bluegill's mouth and said, "I wonder what the rich folks are doing today. I know one thing. Whatever it is, they aren't having more fun than we are."

I agreed and observed that fishing was mighty good medicine, but I needed a lot more doses than my office schedule permitted.

"Yeah," said my fishing buddy. "If everybody went fishing once or twice a week, the psychiatrists wouldn't make enough money to buy groceries."

A few moments after I boated a two-pound largemouth bass that had hit my six-inch purple plastic worm, my friend fooled a bragging-size bream with the little green bug.

Shadows grew longer on the water, the pan fish began feeding on the surface, and my friend picked up a dozen more bluegills that struck a popping bug on his fly rod. He asked a question that I'd heard on a farm pond years ago in south Georgia: "Don't you think the prettiest sound in the world is the 'slurp' the bream makes when he strikes the popping bug?"

The sun had disappeared on the horizon behind the oaks, maples, and sweetgums, and it was time to go home. We had a nice mess of fish, and the day spent in the country had been perfect in every way. You can't possibly put a price tag on the great value of a day on a lake or river. It's sort of like visiting in heaven for a few precious hours.

Outwit 'Em With a Glow

A number of fly fishermen have had glowing success on farm ponds down in south Georgia each summer for several years. They are fishing with popping bugs that glow in the dark, and the big, old bluegills and shellcrackers are crazy about this addition to the late-supper menu.

When Revenal Winge of Waycross, Georgia, told me about this method of fishing, I thought at first he was kidding. However, I remembered that Revenal is very serious about things of a piscatorial nature, so I quit laughing and listened.

"This is what they're using," he said. "It's a white popping bug with black hackle and white streamers, and it's made by Marathon Tackle up in Mosinee, Wisconsin."

On the card the lure was simply identified as "popping bug," and I noticed it had a No. 6 hook and would be suitable not only for large bream but also for fair-sized largemouth bass.

"Remember to take along a lantern or flashlight when you're using this bug at night," said Revenal. "You can shine a two-cell flashlight on the bug, and it glows in the dark. Fish with it a little while, and when the glow starts fading, turn on the flashlight again. Some of the fishermen would rather fish only in moonlight, because on a dark night you can't see where to throw it and you'd get hung up on bushes. They're really catching monstrous bream. A man came in the other day and said he had caught 13 bream that weighed a total of 12 pounds. That's big bream."

Most of these nocturnal anglers work the popping bugs with fly rods close to banks of farm ponds; others use cane or fiberglass poles.

"If you're using a bug pole," said Revenal, "you'll want about 12-pound test line and three or four more feet of line than the pole's length. It throws easier than a fly rod, and you can drop it in a tiny pocket or behind a stump or roots. Shake that bug one time, the bream will hit it, and you come over the stump with him."

Fishing with popping bugs is very productive in south Georgia and north Florida ponds and rivers from the middle of March until the first frost.

"Usually the less you move that bug on the water, the bigger fish you will catch," said Revenal. "But sometimes you may have to trot that bug across the water."

Wayne Papini of Marathon Tackle told me that the lure has been made since the late 1940s. The enameled cork body floats high on the water and is noted for its durability.

"When we slot or cut the body to put the hook in, we glue the hook in, but then take a nylon thread and wrap the hook in it," he said. "It comes in hook sizes from No. 16 to 1-ought. Color patterns include chartreuse and black, off-color yellow and black, and the black and white."

Papini said some fishermen in North Carolina and South Carolina fish 2½ feet of line on cane poles in rivers and "recharge" the bug with lanterns, making it glow for almost three minutes.

This luminous popping bug also is quite effective when fished next to banks, around brush, and next to stumps and logs during that magic period, twilight time, when pan fish and bass rise to the surface to feed on insects.

I can't help but wonder if luminous paint would make a topwater bass plug more appealing. Maybe a glowing plastic worm would attract the attention of largemouth and spotted bass. Don't laugh. I'd bait my hook with a piece of banana peeling coated with luminous paint if I thought a fish would strike it.

II
Largemouth Bass

Greg Rowland, 13, cast artificial lures in a farm pond and caught these two giant largemouth bass, each weighing over 12 pounds, in the same morning, a feat regarded as quite incredible by folks still looking for their first 10-pounder.

Greatest Freshwater Game Fish

Shortly before my 12th birthday in June, 1945, Dad handed me his level-wind baitcasting reel, invited me to step into the front yard and announced, "I'm going to teach you how to cast, and beginning next Saturday I will give you some lessons in bass fishing."

I cast several hours with a practice plug that week, pretending a bass was lying next to a tree. Don't ask me how many backlashes I untangled. Dad taught me to cast with "an educated thumb" lightly touching the turning spool as the lure traveled through the air. Slowly but surely I learned the overhand, sidearm, and backhand casts, and was pleased to note my accuracy improving.

On Saturday we rode a few miles to a farm pond where we spent the morning walking along the banks and casting shallow-running artificial lures. After two minor backlashes and at least 25 casts, I caught a one-pound largemouth bass that struck a wiggling plug called the River Runt.

The yearling bass bent the limber steel rod enough to excite me, leaped completely out of the water, and refused to quit fighting until I had pulled it onto the grassy bank. This scrappy young fish helped make my blossoming case of fishing fever much more serious—absolutely incurable, in fact.

In 1947, my parents and I moved to Waycross, Georgia, where my father, J. D. Salter, became the city school superintendent.

During my high school and college years, I spent dozens of Saturdays fishing with Dad in a 14½-foot plywood johnboat in south Georgia farm ponds, the Satilla River, St. Marys River, and the Okefenokee Swamp. He was my best pal, my favorite fishing partner, and a versatile and consistently successful angler.

Up to that point we had been casting glass-eyed, wooden, shallow-running plugs, topwater lures, silver spoons with pork rind, and rubber-skirted baits with spinning silver blades.

Then in the 1950s, a revolution occurred in black bass fishing. Soft plastic worms designed to imitate eels, baby snakes, or salamanders became available. The worms, sometimes displayed in glass jars in hardware stores and fish bait shops, cost about 15 cents each. Dad saw the possibilities in this bait and began using the worms in 1956 or 1957.

Fishermen used one or two hooks in the worm's body. They either retrieved it slowly to imitate a swimming eel or snake, or they sank it with split shot pinched on the line or with aid of a sliding sinker and dragged it on the lake bottom.

My father preferred the swimming method of worming in the shallow lakes, and he decided a longer bait would offer better action and attract bigger bass.

Experimenting in his garage at home in Waycross and testing the plastic worms in ponds and rivers in his spare time, he made a lure that largemouth bass simply couldn't resist.

He would buy pairs of plastic worms in the same color pattern, then cut off the head of one and the tail of another, and put them end to end. After heating the blade of a screwdriver on a camping stove, Dad would use the hot metal to fuse the worms, thereby making a longer bait. Then he reheated the screwdriver and smoothed the joint.

He would push the barb of a 2-ought hook through the worm's head and one, sometimes two, other hooks through the body, then link them with strong braided line. The worms usually were seven to nine inches in length.

"This longer plastic worm has more action," he told me. "I

never fish this lure on the bottom of a farm pond or river. I retrieve it at a shallow depth.

"I cast the worm to a target area on the shoreline—a fallen tree, a stump, brush, log, or grass, then let it sink two or three feet. The bass hears and sees this worm sinking, apparently crippled. But, when I begin the retrieve and twitch the rod tip on each turn of the reel handle, the worm appears to recover and swim away. Ninety percent of the strikes will come only a short distance from where the lure first hit the water."

Although the bass in Georgia ponds still found the shallow-swimming worms quite appealing during the summer, these lures were even more effective in the spring and fall. In the spring it wasn't uncommon for a curious bass to follow the swimming bait all the way to the boat and lunge at the worm when it was four or five feet from the rod's tip.

Revenal Winge of Waycross, one of my father's old friends, recalls that one of Dad's first successful, "surgically improved" worms had a red body with a pale, lime-green streak down the top.

"He mixed the colors in the next several years to get good color combinations, but I think he always believed red was the best."

I also remember seeing Dad catch largemouths on his plastic worms in color patterns of red and white, green and white, black and yellow, and white with black spots.

His biggest catch on these worms was a bass weighing slightly over ten pounds, and the largemouths in the five- to eight-pound class numbered in the dozens. It wasn't unusual for him to land his daily limit—15 at that time. I once saw him pull a total of 27 bass out of a small lake in an afternoon of casting, and he released all except a nice mess for a family fish fry.

One of his friends, Mac McClelland, used one of Dad's plastic worms to catch a 12½-pound bass in a south Georgia lake, and another friend, R. L. Walker, boated numerous trophies that hit the fake eels in the Satilla River.

I well remember how Dad's white plastic worm with little black spots was a sensation in the St. Marys River and also in the Little St. Marys River near Kingsland in southeast Georgia.

"One day bass were feeding in the mouth of a creek that flows out of rice fields into the Little St. Marys," he told me in 1960. "I made a cast and turned the reel's handle only once. Old Newt grabbed that plastic worm and headed the other way toward Tallahassee. I never could turn him.

"If there is a little trick in fusing these worms to achieve the proper action, there is also a trick in retrieving it properly. A slow to medium speed, straight retrieve draws an occasional strike, but the best method is to twitch the rod tip on each turn of the reel's handle, a rhythm that gives the worm a wiggling, lifelike swimming action. I have never used a lure which would attract bass so consistently."

A heart attack forced my father to retire early in 1963, and he died at the age of 58 in January, 1966, while fishing with a friend on a south Georgia farm pond. They had caught 25 crappie before he was stricken and died suddenly in the johnboat.

* * *

For more than 25 years, my father enjoyed terrific success in topwater bass fishing with a Creek Chub Darter in the silver flash pattern. The wooden bait with an open mouth and three treble hooks was a superb imitation of an injured baitfish.

In the early 1960s, he switched to the Rapala, a slender, balsa, cigar-shaped lure carved in Finland; a plastic lip gave it a shallow running retrieve. In the black-and-silver and also the black-and-gold pattern, the Rapala was the greatest surface bait of them all, according to my father. One spring he caught a total of 150 bass on one black-and-silver Rapala, then gave it to a friend because the lures were scarce.

"Before you ever become a good fisherman with surface lures, you must develop more patience and slow down," he cautioned me one morning as we fished in his johnboat on a farm pond. "You're working that lure too fast.

"Remember you are trying to imitate a crippled minnow. A small fish that has been injured won't be seen racing across the surface. The minnow is struggling to escape from a predator such as a bass, and he will make a short movement, pause and rest on the surface, and then struggle to move again. This slowly moving, crippled fish looks like an easy prey for a bass."

He added, "Unless the action is perfectly natural, a bass won't strike. The same is true when you are fly fishing with a popping bug. Remember how slowly an insect moves on the water, making small ripples as he inches along, stops, and moves again."

One of his ten commandments of bass angling was "Don't waste casts in unproductive water." He was a target caster, choosing to present his bait around logs, stumps, brush, grass, and treetops, where bass likely would be lurking in ambush for a baitfish.

Several months before his death, we were casting the Rapala and Jim Bagley's Bang-O-Lure, which Dad also regarded as an exceptionally good surface lure.

"I've had a lot of luck with the black lure with silver sides," he observed, "but since it's so cloudy, I believe the darker one, black back and gold sides, will be better. The bass can more easily see the darker silhouette against the overcast sky."

On a bright sunny day, he usually cast brightly colored surface and underwater lures. He didn't fish at night, but he recommended a very dark, even a black plug that he felt would present a better silhouette against the starry sky.

Shortly before sundown on a spring day, he suggested, "A bass may be lying next to that stump. Cast beyond the stump, and slowly work the lure back toward it. You'll attract his attention best this way. A cast very close to the stump occasionally will spook a fish.

"You will frighten a bass by making a noise, by bumping the boat, or dropping your pliers. Shadows cast on the water also will spook a bass. When possible, face the sun when you cast so that the shadow of the lure going through the air won't fall on the water close to the fish and frighten him. I have seen bass spooked by the shadow of a lure before the lure hits the water."

Dad also thought it was foolish to wear a white shirt while casting lures in shallow water. Sunlight reflected by the white cloth might scare a bass lying next to the bank.

Dad believed that the St. Marys River in southeast Georgia was the most beautiful stream that the good Lord ever created, and he took me numerous times to Charlie Merck's fishing camp near Kingsland.

On my first trip to the St. Marys, I asked the former railroad worker, "Mr. Merck, what're the bass biting?"

He removed a plug from his tackle box and said, "I've caught a few on this frog popper this week."

In the palm of his hand he held a wooden surface plug made by Creek Chub that looked like a baitfish with its mouth open. When new, the lure had a frog finish on the back and a yellow concave belly with two treble hooks. The concave belly made it lie naturally on the top of the water, and when the rod tip was jerked a bit to give it crippled baitfish action, the lure wouldn't move far. It sort of hugged the surface.

The chipped, battle-scarred plug didn't have a single fleck of paint left on it.

"All the paint's gone," I observed in my youthful innocence. "Do the fish really still strike it?"

Mr. Merck smiled and replied, "That doesn't make any difference. It's not particularly the color, it's the action of the plug that gets a fish's attention. He doesn't care what color it is as long as it looks like a crippled minnow, what he'd call an easy meal.

"The paint's been off a long time, but when they're hungry, the bass will come after it. This is the fifth set of treble hooks I've had on this frog popper. I've caught at least five hundred bass on this plug."

His advice for fishing a topwater plug is just as important to follow today as it was in 1949: "Be patient, fish a surface plug slowly so it'll look natural, and always keep a tight line."

In the ensuing years, I caught a lot of largemouths with a "cut-out, yellow-bellied frog Darter."

"Get the Net, Honey"

If Jessie Cunningham of Madison, Georgia, had become a bass tournament fisherman instead of continuing her work as a visiting teacher, she probably would have collected a small fortune.

A 12 lb. 2 oz. black bass hangs on the wall in her den, and keeping it company are a couple of 10 lb. 4 oz. lunkers. She has lost count of the bass weighing between 5 and 9 pounds that have struck her lures.

She has given away to neighbors more trophy fish than most bass anglers land in a lifetime.

Her husband, Charles Cunningham, retired Madison postmaster, is proud of his mounted 10-pound bass that hit a Heddon Lucky 13 on the surface and another 10-pounder that he took on a plastic worm. He, too, has made the neighbors happy by presenting them with bass for the frying pan or oven.

Perhaps his most memorable bass was an 8½-pounder that struck a popping bug and fought like a tiger 30 minutes until finally being worn to a frazzle by a fly rod.

Jessie's 12 lb. 2 oz. lunker was taken on a Big Daddy Fliptail plastic worm in a farm pond near Madison late one afternoon in June, 1969.

"He hit it very lightly," she said. "I thought it was a tiny bass. Charles said, 'Be careful and don't pull it out of his mouth.' When I set the hook, the rod bent, and the bass jumped like a porpoise. And when I saw it, I got shaky. I finally played the bass back to the boat. When we got ready to put a net under it, the fish ran under the boat and the rod hit against the side of the boat."

After the bass was put into the boat, Jessie, Charles, and their friend, Vic Johnson, saw evidence that she had kept a tight line all the way.

"The hook fell out of the fish's mouth," she said. "I had set the hook, but the fish's lip was so big the barb didn't get through. We put the bass in the boat's live well, and I tried to be calm and fish some more. But the fish jumped while I was sitting on the top of the live well, and I got so scared I almost jumped out, and I was as white as a sheet."

Charles and Jessie Cunningham said they received lessons in bass fishing about 20 years ago from the late Zeke Biggers of Madison, who, they agree, was indeed a very remarkable bass angler.

Biggers got a big kick out of catching lunker-class bass, but he seemed to derive even more satisfaction from teaching his friends how to fool America's greatest freshwater game fish.

A friendly, selfless man with a keen sense of humor, Biggers was a cotton broker for a number of years; he died at the age of 63 in 1975.

He told me in 1969, that he needed only three lures to catch a mess of bass, but he didn't necessarily use all three in the same day.

"I like a topwater lure, a black Fliptail plastic worm, and the white thing," he said. "February and March have been my best months for bass. Three or four days of sunshine sometimes make them stir around before spring starts."

The "white thing" was a minnow-like lure named the Shark Ike, a small, sinking white bait with red eyes, a dorsal fin, and two sets of treble hooks.

"When the water is still cold in the ponds, I throw it as far as I can out in that deep water and reel it back fast," said Biggers. "It throws like a bullet."

One winter afternoon he and Cunningham cast Shark Ikes from the bank of a small pond, and he hooked a bass that some of us have hunted for years.

"I cast the white thing far out in water that was ten feet deep, and the bass struck about half-way back," said Biggers. "It was a hard strike. I call that kind of hit a shoulder jiggler."

The bass didn't jump out of the cold water, but she boiled twice on the surface and took line several times from Biggers, who was using a Johnson Saber closed-face reel, 6½-foot rod and 12-pound test line.

"I was standing on the edge of the water and pulled the bass right up on the grass," Biggers said. "It weighed 11 pounds, 4 ounces."

On a wall of his Madison home hang two mounted bass that he caught eight years apart, a 13-pounder and a 10 lb. 10 oz. beauty.

"They say this plug makes sound in the water," said Biggers. "Maybe bass are attracted to underwater sound. I don't believe they see color, but if the sun is shining they can see something coming and strike at it.

"You'll catch your biggest bass in February and March while they are carrying eggs. The best time to go fishing is every chance you get. Go where the fish are, and keep the lure in the water.

"I like a little ripple on the water when I'm bass fishing," he added. "There's been a ripple on the surface every time I've caught a big bass. I like for the wind to blow in my face. Then the fish come toward you as they are feeding."

Biggers offered a tip on setting the hook when a bass picks up a plastic worm.

"I learned from the oldtimers fishing with live minnows," he said. "A fish hits a minnow and carries the bobber under. The bobber later comes to the top. Then it goes down the second time, and you set the hook. With a plastic worm, a fisherman should let him run with it a little. Mrs. Cunningham is a real good bass fisherman, and I've seen her wait five to ten minutes, it seemed like, after a bass takes the worm before she sets the hook."

Charles Cunningham said that Biggers was almost totally blind for several months before his death. But, he continued to fish, and he caught more lunkers than most anglers who have 20-20 vision.

"One day he caught a bass that weighed 10 pounds, 10 ounces, and he had it mounted simply because he caught it when he was blind," said Charles. Biggers' biggest bass was over 13 pounds.

Biggers fished with closed-face Johnson reels and nothing stronger than 12-pound test line, and he took most of his trophy bass on nine-inch black or purple Fliptail worms in farm ponds. Among his favorite plugs were the Heddon Sonic, Shark Ike, Hot Spot, Lucky 13, Thunderbird, ThinFin, and Rapala.

Teenager Lands Two "Hawgs"

A very high percentage of America's over sixty million fishermen never have landed a seven-pound black bass. One of my best friends has been fishing 45 to 48 weekends each year since 1969, and he's still two ounces shy of the ten-pound mark for bass.

He almost fainted when I told him that a 13-year-old Wrightsville, Georgia, boy caught two bass weighing over 12 pounds each in an hour and 45 minutes.

Young Greg Rowland, who had been earning money mowing lawns in the summer of 1979, checked the solunar tables and noticed that a major feeding period for game and fish would occur early on the morning of July 6. The alarm clock awoke him very early, and he rode his bicycle two miles to the lake with tackle box tied on the back bumper and rod and reel in hand. He was fishing by 6:30 A.M.

The boy remembered what Jack Wingate had taught him at the boys camp on Lake Seminole three years earlier, and he tied a topwater plug on his line, hoping a big bass would feed before the sun's rays touched the water.

"I was standing on the dam, and I threw out the Devil's Horse, the one that is yellow with green stripes, and gave it short jerks," said Greg. "Just enough to make a little bit of noise. Then I let it sit still a while and jerked it again."

In the deep water near the dam, an old, fat, hungry

bucketmouth thought she spotted an easy breakfast, a crippled fish struggling on the surface.

"The bass hit it real good, and it scared me because I wasn't expecting it," the boy said. "I set the hook, and my rod started bending so much, I felt it was a pretty good-size fish.

"I let her go, and she went off to my left, and sort of half-jumped and stuck her head out of the water. It scared me when I saw how big the fish was. I was afraid I would lose her if she ran by some rocks around the dam."

At that moment, his parents, Mr. and Mrs. Hodges Rowland, probably were sipping coffee back home and wondering if their son had had a bite yet.

"Once I got her close to the bank and reached down to pick her up, I didn't have a good place to grab her lip, because all three sets of treble hooks were in her mouth," said Greg. "I grabbed her fast by the lower lip."

The huge largemouth bass weighed 12 lb. 4 oz. The youngster picked up his fish stringer and snapped three of the safety pin rings through the fish's lower lip and secured her in a shallow spot at the bank.

"I was really shook up after catching that big bass," said Greg, little dreaming that a monster that could have been that giant's twin sister would strike less than two hours later.

"I was fishing off the dam again and had tied on a nine-inch black plastic worm, a Fliptail," he said. "I threw the worm in that deep water and sort of gave it little jerks with the rod and let it sit on the bottom, then pulled it slowly."

Suddenly, he felt the familiar tap, tap of a fish picking up the worm.

Greg said, "I felt it sort of hit a little bit, and I gave it slack. The fish started taking out line, and I set the hook, and she really took off and felt as big as the first fish. The bass came around to my left, and she came up and rolled on the surface."

Within a couple of minutes the boy grabbed the lower lip of a 12 lb. 3 oz. bass.

Fishing with a Johnson Century closed-face reel and 17-

pound Stren monofilament line, Greg hooked two more large bass, but each broke off.

The boy's father arrived at the pond and asked whether he had had any luck. Greg, trying to keep from grinning, replied, "Not much." He reached for the stringer, picked up the fish and was thrown off balance by their weight and fell on the bank.

Mrs. Rowland told me, "Greg has been an ardent fisherman since he was a toddler, and has always possessed an attribute that every good fisherman must have—patience."

The two humongous bass were mounted by a taxidermist and displayed on a wall in the Rowland home next to an 8 lb. 4 oz. bass that Greg had caught on a Super Shad plug the previous January.

When asked to give other anglers a tip so they might learn how to hook a trophy bass, Greg smiled and replied, "I'm not but 13 years old, and I can't give any advice to grown people."

Phillip's World-Record Catch

Alabama's picturesque, 21,000-acre Lewis Smith Lake near Jasper is beyond any doubt the South's best reservoir for trophy-class spotted bass, yielding the last five world records for this close relative of the largemouth. In 1972, Billy Henderson of Birmingham shattered the mark with an 8 lb. 10½ oz. spotted bass.

In April, 1979, Phillip C. Terry, Jr., 15, of Decatur, Alabama, was notified by the International Game Fish Association that his 8 lb. 15 oz. spotted bass taken the previous year was recognized as a world record.

Boated in Smith Lake, March 18, 1978, the fish's species went unrecognized while the boy was earning money to have it mounted. The frozen fish was taken to a taxidermist that July, and when Phillip picked up his trophy in December, he was told it certainly resembled a spotted bass.

An Alabama fisheries biologist examined the bass and concluded it might be a spot. Dr. John S. Ramsey of Auburn University later was shown the fish and identified it as a spotted bass. The Alabama teenager submitted his application to the I.G.F.A., waited a number of suspenseful weeks for a decision and finally received the good news April 16, 1979.

Phillip was working at a food market and preparing to enroll in the tenth grade when I telephoned him for details about that memorable March day on Smith Lake.

The water temperature was in the mid-40s, the sky was cloudy and a slight breeze rippled the surface. Around 11 A.M., Phillip's father, hopping a ½-ounce black and chartreuse spinnerbait along the rocky bottom, pulled out an 8 lb. 3 oz. largemouth bass. The boy tied on a black- and yellow-spinnerbait, which he allowed to sink to the bottom, raised his rod tip 12 o'clock high and let the bait sink with the spinner blade turning.

"The water was 20 to 25 feet deep," said Phillip. "I played the spinnerbait slowly and pumped the rod and let it fall. That fish hit once and didn't get hooked, then struck again, and on the third lick I set the hook hard. It sounded deeper and stayed down on the bottom. It never really jumped. When I pulled it close to the boat, the bass rolled on the surface."

When the bass was boated a moment later, the boy's father admired it and remarked, "It would be something if that was a spotted bass."

One of Phillip's fishing friends later was excited when the teenager opened the freezer and showed him the big fish. But, weeks were to pass before Phillip was told by the taxidermist that it well could be a spot.

The bass was weighed on certified meat scales in a store the day it was caught, and it was 25½ inches long with an 18½-inch girth.

Phillip and his father fish Smith Lake often, and their most productive artificial lures have been six-inch brown or chartreuse plastic worms and either black-and-yellow or black-and-chartreuse spinnerbaits. Their best months for bass are October, November, March, and April.

A Fountain of Youth

A Georgia electrician received a strong, shoulder-jarring jolt on Easter Sunday 1980, that left him smiling from ear to ear and feeling considerably younger than his 68 years. J. D. Gray of Mableton, Georgia, wasn't being careless in his work, mind you. Actually, he had been trying nearly 31 years to enjoy such a piscatorially shocking experience.

A prince of a gentleman and a charter member of the South Cobb Bass Club, Gray told me that back in 1949, on Lake Cornelius in the mountains of Puerto Rico, he used a topwater plug to catch an 11 lb. 8 oz. largemouth bass. For the next three decades he tried to outwit an even heavier bass, but the goal appeared to be increasingly elusive.

"All those years, I've traveled thousands of miles, going from lake to lake, even out to Texas and Oklahoma, looking for that fish," he said. "I finally caught it in Lake Hartwell on my homemade spinnerbait."

He cast his chartreuse-skirted lure with a brass blade into 25 feet of water and began slowly pulling it up a ledge, working the bait like a plastic worm.

"My friend Charles Redding taught me how to fish a spinnerbait on the bottom and crawl it like a worm," he said. "The lure hit something on the ledge, and I let it fall back, then saw the line running in the water, and I set the hook hard. The bass came to the top, and it looked like it tailwalked 50 feet. The fish ran under the boat and fought nearly ten minutes before we got him in the net. That bass weighed 12 pounds, 6 ounces."

The lure—let's call it the J. D. Special—was made even more appealing by sticking a frog-colored pork chunk on the hook.

"I've caught several hundred bass on these spinnerbaits since I started making them in 1979," he said. "I make them out of smaller gauge wire, and this gives the lure more vibrations. Put on a frog pork chunk, and it vibrates real good and jumps up and down. I had on another bass that weighed about five pounds, but it got off. I've got several bass weighing eight pounds or more on my wall, and I got them on this spinnerbait, too."

On a bright, spring day while two friends and I were frying fish on the bank of a cove in Georgia's 11,860-acre Lake Allatoona, I saw Gray, fishing alone, approaching in his bass boat and casting a small crankbait to the rocky shoreline. We asked if he'd had any luck. "I've got ten bass, but there's no size to 'em."

He was casting a little Humpback Rebel, a long-lipped, diving plug that resembles a threadfin shad, on an ultralight spinning outfit with eight-pound test line. The plug had very few flecks of gold and black paint left.

I laughed and asked about the plug's battle scars. Gray said, "I've caught more than a hundred bass on this lure since January 1." A year later he confided that a bass snapped his line and ran away with the lure after he had counted more than two hundred bass that struck it in reservoirs.

"When I'm fishing the Humpback Rebel in Allatoona, I start it off fast and slow it down when I think it's down close to the bottom. Largemouths and spots will strike it. I've got some bass up to seven pounds on it.

"When I am by myself, I parallel the bank with a lure. I get 25 or 30 feet out and move down the bank. When you are by yourself, you will catch more fish. I can cover a lot more territory that I think the fish are in. When somebody is with me, we get out a ways and both of us throw to the bank."

He enjoys fishing surface lures for bass, but the majority of his fish are taken on medium to deep-running plugs that resemble threadfin shad. He also takes a lot of bass on plastic worms. In the spring, autumn, and winter, he works his lures on points and banks, and then fishes deep water with plastic worms in the summer.

In the early spring when the water still is a bit dingy, he likes to fish with a six-inch purple Creme worm with a red tail, and he uses a ½-ounce sliding sinker, a strong, sharp hook, 17- to 20-pound test line, freespool baitcasting reel, and very stiff rod.

"I fish that firetail worm for spotted bass," he said. "When I get a tap, tap, I just let it lie there a minute and let him take it. When I see my line start moving, I hit him. I noticed a boy with me in my boat last year would get a tap, tap; he'd try to set the hook immediately and wouldn't catch him. I'd get a tap, let it lie there, watch my line, see it moving and hit him. He asked, 'How is it that you get one every time it hits, and I don't?'"

Gray told him the secret of worming for spotted bass, and he followed the advice and began hooking the wary, tricky spots.

"I like to fish topwater with a Dying Flutter," said Gray. "I usually lay it as close as I can beside a bush or under a bush. I just flutter it right out. I pause and work it real slowly. Hugh Worley and I used to go to Clarks Hill, and we'd tear 'em up with Dying Flutters."

Does he believe that the moon has much effect on the fish and their feeding habits?

"I sure do," he said. "I like the dark of the moon. If I was going to fish at night—and I don't really like night fishing—I'd want a dark night. I've caught bass early and late, and I've caught big fish on topwater plugs right in the middle of the day with the weather real hot. The afternoon is probably the best time, though."

Spoon-Jigging in Winter

Many southern bass anglers used to put away their fishing tackle after the first frost and not make another cast until just before the dogwoods bloomed in spring. A few avid anglers, however, bundled up in heavy clothing, tied on a jig and eel and fished for largemouth and spotted bass in the cold water of deep, clear reservoirs.

Others were casting shiny silver spoons and hopping them across the bottom with moderate success. In the 1960s, a very small number of fishermen simply dropped silver spoons right off the side of the boat and jigged them vertically on the bottom. These spoon-jiggers put bass on their stringers, and they didn't do much talking about this technique of bassin'.

In the autumn and winter of 1970, and in 1971, word slowly leaked out, and members of bass clubs affiliated with Bass Anglers Sportsman Society started jigging spoons under their boats and catching largemouths, smallmouths, and spots in tournaments each month.

This method of fishing can make a fisherman as bored as a guy watching paint dry or as busy as a cat scrambling on a hot tin roof. Depends on whether or not they are biting.

Eddie Withrow, a Greyhound bus-driver who resides in Lula, Georgia, close to the banks of the Chattahoochee River and a few miles above Lake Sidney Lanier, has enjoyed spoon-jigging for bass in autumn and winter in the 38,000-acre impoundment for ten years.

The season for this angling method begins in early October and continues until about the first week in March, and fish usually bite best when the water temperature ranges from the high 40s to the low 50s, although a few have been hooked when sheets of ice covered the shoreline.

Eddie fishes with a freespool baitcasting reel, a medium to heavy action graphite or a boron rod, and 14-pound test monofilament line. The spoons range in weight from ⅜ of an ounce to a full ounce.

When he's running his outboard motor, Eddie uses a depth finder on the console of his bass boat to find deep-water habitat favored by bass; when he turns on his electric trolling motor, he uses a depth finder on the bow to check an area for suitable structure.

The structure reminds you of summertime worming holes, except they often are a bit deeper. Eddie sometimes finds bass lying on submerged islands, on edges of creek channels, off deep points, on rocky ledges, around brush and fallen trees, and at the base of standing timber or suspended in its branches.

In early autumn he hooks bass at 12 to 25 feet, but in the winter he has caught them at 40 to 68 feet.

Eddie said some spoons flutter slowly to the bottom and may have a tendency to twist the line unless a swivel is used. He prefers to tie the line directly to the O-ring in a spoon that sinks like a rock right beside the boat, dropping the bait straight onto the structure he has spotted seconds earlier on the depth finder.

"In the winter there is a threadfin shad kill, or dieoff. When the water gets very cold, and the bass sees the spoon falling, and he thinks it is a crippled or dying shad," he said, "he'll strike the spoon on the fall.

"Early in the autumn the strikes may be vicious, but in the winter a majority of the time you won't feel the bass hit that way. You raise the spoon off the bottom, let it fall, and right then he hits it, and you raise it again and feel some pressure or a little tap. Or, when you let it fall again, the line goes slack, and the fish is there and has it in his mouth."

Because the strike often is so light at great depths, a fisherman must be a very observant line-watcher, he cautioned.

"When spooning season starts, they put up a good fight, but in the winter they are sluggish in that cold water. Catch a bass from a depth of 40 feet or more in winter, and you might as well plan to put him in the ice chest. The change in pressure hurts him, and his eyeballs bulge out."

Release a bass taken from 40 to 55 feet of water, and it either dies very soon, or it appears disoriented, lying on the side or back, unable to swim away.

"Normally you will find that bass single out one tree and stay around it," he said. "One day you find the bass at the base of the tree trunk, the next week they might be suspended halfway up in branches, and at other times they may be in the top of the tree.

"You'll see the tree and branches make your depth finder light up with a lot of blips like a Christmas tree. Some may be fish. Sit there in the boat. If the wind's not blowing, and you see blips move or go on and off, you know it's fish, because, like Tom Mann said, the limbs don't move."

When Eddie determines the depth at which suspended bass are lying in a tree top, he drops his spoon into the water and counts the number of times the reel's line carriage moves the full width of the spool. Depending upon the size of the baitcasting reel, six to eight feet of line will come off the spool on each trip of the line carriage across it.

"The biggest spots I've caught jigging spoons weighed 4½ to 5 pounds," he said. "My best day ever in spooning, my partner and I caught a little over one hundred bass, the biggest going 8 pounds."

During his youth in West Virginia and on trips back home as an adult, Eddie has enjoyed fishing for smallmouth bass in streams with hair jigs, jigs and pork rind strips, and small, diving crankbaits.

"When I was a kid, we fished with the jig and rind, better known back home as the fly 'n rind," he said. "I cast it out, let it go to the bottom, and fish it very slowly like a plastic worm, dragging it on the bottom or hopping it. It's a funny bite when the smallmouth hits. It may feel like the lure is in moss, just a little pressure, but he's got it in his mouth."

Eddie believes the smallmouth bass is the greatest freshwater game fish, a rugged fighter that, when hooked, immediately goes to the surface, leaps like a tarpon and tailwalks, shaking its head trying to throw the lure.

"I remember catching them on a small bait, the Potato Bug lure," he said. "It was silver and had a bright orange back with black dots. A four-inch, split-tailed brown or black eel was good, too. In crankbaits, use the crawfish pattern or the shad color. The Mister Twister Sassy Shad with the wiggling tail and Tom Mann's Swimmin' Grub are good smallmouth baits, too."

Several of Eddie's friends used to kid him about releasing the big bass that were the stars of his tall fishing tales. One said, "When are you going to show us some evidence when you tell about a string of bass that included a real hoss, a big mama?"

Eddie chuckled and said, "All right, boys. Go ahead and laugh. But in December, I'm going to catch a hawg in Lake Lanier."

On a Sunday morning in December 1972, he was fishing with Mike Strong in a Lanier Bass Club tournament. Eddie figured a lunker might be in slightly stained water in a cove in upper reaches of Lake Lanier. The boat was lying over 18 feet of water when he made the memorable cast right on the doorstep of the oldtimer.

"I threw a chrome Little George [a lead-body tailspinner] into a bunch of stickups," he said. "You could see the tops of them. I let it flutter down, and the bass struck before the lure hit the bottom. I felt a slight bump.

"That bass almost pulled the rod and spinning reel out of my hands. When she ran, the drag on that reel was really screaming. I was using 14-pound test line. At first I honestly thought it was maybe a seven-pound bass, a strong, younger fish."

Several minutes later he led into Strong's landing net a handsome, 11 lb. 4 oz. largemouth bass.

"The bass never did jump," he said. "She just bulldogged straight for the bottom. Three times she ran under the boat, and I was afraid she was a goner."

In the previous December, he caught two eight-pound bass in Lanier, so you can't blame him for interrupting his Christmas shopping to jig spoons or work Little Georges on the bottom in that deep, clear lake.

"When I cast the Little George, I keep a tight line, because on the lure's fall, you'll get a lot of strikes," he said. "If I hadn't had a tight line on the fall that day, that big bass might have hit and backed off."

Confidence Is the Best Lure

Several years ago at a class reunion, someone walked up to Mrs. Bill Dance of Memphis and asked, "What does your husband do for a living?"

Mrs. Dance replied, "He fishes."

Dance laughed and said, "People looked at her sideways, not knowing whether to believe it. A lot of people wish all they had to do was fish."

The former Memphis furniture salesman won a number of Bass Anglers Sportsman Society's national bass tournaments in his nearly ten years on the cast-for-cash trail. For several years, he has hosted a weekly television fishing show seen across the nation.

One of the most highly skilled of the new breed of scientific anglers, Dance, 39, is basically a structure fisherman who carefully studies maps of reservoirs, then reads a depth finder to seek out the unknown, the hideaways of bass in deeper water.

"I fish 265 days a year," he said. "You learn every time you go. New things happen. There's not a man alive who catches fish every time he goes. It's a challenge."

In Arkansas Dance has caught bass as deep as 65 feet, and in other states he has had big catches at depths of 20 to 40 feet.

How does he find fish when most anglers on a lake are getting skunked?

"I enjoy fishing underwater structure," he said. "When you

find structure, there is one key place in a given area where a fish can be found. This is the area closest to deeper water.

"Confidence is the best lure in your tackle box. I've got probably five lures that I use a majority of the time and have the most confidence in. They are a plastic worm, a jig and eel, a spoon, a weighted tailspin bait, and a spinnerbait."

He added, "If you find an island, it may slope in 75 to 90 percent of the area. Somewhere on the island there is a quick drop in depth. This seems to be the most productive place. About 80 percent of the bass I catch are always close to deeper water. The instinct of a bass to be next to deep water applies. The fish might even be in water only five feet deep, but there's deep water nearby."

Finding a large number of fish in a deep-water sanctuary is as satisfying to Dance as actually catching them, and he frequently releases trophy-class bass.

Dance, who learned to fish at the age of six in Tennessee creeks, believes the smallmouth bass is the greatest fighter in fresh water, with the spotted bass ranking second and the largemouth third. His favorite lake is Tennessee's Pickwick Lake, where an angler can catch all three species of bass. His preferences for largemouths are Sam Rayburn reservoir in Texas and Georgia's Walter F. George and Seminole.

When asked to name his favorite color in plastic worms, Dance smiled and said, "Color makes no difference, just as long as it's blue."

But, he explained in a serious vein, "I fish five basic colors of plastic worms. I fish green, the avocado, in off-colored, murky water. And I've had real good luck on black, and I fish blue, violet, and red. I primarily concentrate on dark colors such as violet and black at night.

"I guess in mid-day fishing, I use blue worms 90 percent of the time. Early and late and on cloudy days, I fish violet or black. I have seen the time when the color made all the difference in the world."

The next time you go fishing for black bass, just remember this statement by Bill Dance:

"Confidence is the greatest lure in anybody's tackle box. Having confidence in his ability, believing in what he is doing, and having confidence in his equipment and lure selections are important. I always believe I'm gonna catch a fish on every cast."

Bill says, "If a lure is presented in the proper way, resembling what the fish is accustomed to eating in that season or time of the day, I think he will hit it."

Country Boy's Instinct

J. L. "Junior" Collis, Jr., of Decatur, Georgia, drives a truck to earn a living, and he fishes virtually every Saturday and Sunday of the year because he's driven by an unrelenting obsession to catch black bass. I suspect that when Junior tries to go to sleep each night, he counts jumping bass, and his first thought each morning of his life is, "What'll they hit today—and where?"

Fishing is not only fun and exciting for the 52-year-old Georgian, but also is frequently rewarding in dollars. In the past 12 years he has won numerous bass tournaments on Georgia reservoirs, ranked high in many others and has hooked the first-place prize in a national tournament—the Bass Anglers Sportsman Society contest in 1973, on Lake Keowee in South Carolina.

Junior's major goal in life is to catch a largemouth bass bigger than the world record 22 lb. 4 oz. "hawg" that the late George Perry pulled out of little Montgomery Lake near Lumber City, Georgia, in June, 1932.

This friendly, easy-going bassin' man was born in Gravelly Gap, a suburb of Blue Ridge, in the north Georgia mountains, and he caught his first string of bass on a Creek Chub Pikie in beautiful Blue Ridge Lake.

Junior has taught me a great deal of patience in fishing with plastic worms for bass, and he has helped me to detect the very light pickups that I would have missed if I hadn't been especially observant.

He prefers the Texas rig with plastic worms, running the barb of the hook ¼ inch into the worm's head, bringing the point back out and pushing the eye onto the top of the worm, then turning the hook around and imbedding the barb into the bait's body. This makes the worm weedless and enables you to pull it across rocks, brush, and limbs without hanging up—well, most of the time. A sliding sinker permits longer casts and, of course, takes the worm to the bottom.

"You want a sliding sinker," said Junior, "because when the bass picks up the worm, he moves off and the line goes through the sinker. If the bass felt that sinker, it wouldn't be natural, and he'd spit that worm out."

Junior fishes with worms on a baitcasting rod and reel with 14- to 20-pound test line and a spinning reel with 10- to 14-pound test line. He likes a 6- to 6½-foot heavy-medium to worm-action (very stiff) fiberglass and graphite rod.

He moves the worm by slowly raising the rod tip, making the fake eel or nightcrawler crawl and hop across the bottom next to bushes, stumps, fallen trees, standing timber, docks, and boat houses. The strike may feel like a light tap or a hard thump, but sometimes the line merely goes slack if the fish runs toward the boat. Often the pickup may feel only like pressure on the line, as if the worm is hung in moss.

"When in doubt, set the hook as hard as you can," said Junior. "It doesn't cost anything to jerk it. When you feel something, point that rod tip close to the water, take up your slack, and stick it to him. Like John Powell says, 'Try to cross his eyeballs.'"

He has experimented with numerous colors and sizes of plastic worms over the years in efforts to catch Old Nelly and her mighty, fat grandma. His largest catches have come on black, purple, black-grape, and blue worms. In a clear lake, such as Lanier, he will work a chartreuse, watermelon, or red worm. On some days the bass won't hit a thing but a purple worm with a bright red tail, he finds.

Junior has convinced me that if a person merely wants to

catch a lot of bass, fish running from one to three pounds, he should throw a six-inch worm. An eight- or nine-inch worm will attract fewer strikes, but the bass generally will be considerably bigger. However, there are exceptions, Junior admits, and he has taken some lunkers, bragging-size bigmouths, that inhaled short worms.

Junior's 1973 victory on Lake Keowee came in one of the toughest challenges for the fishing pros in the history of Bass Anglers Sportsman Society. In three days of competition, 162 anglers managed to land only 261 keeper-size bass weighing 761 lb. 3 oz. Junior wound up with six bass that totalled 23 lb. 15 oz. On the opening day he brought in four bass weighing 17 lb. 12 oz. to take the lead, but went fishless the second round and dropped into second place.

He picked up two more bass in the third day of competition and won the tournament by a one-pound margin.

Junior's biggest fish, a 9 lb. 9 oz. bass that struck an eight-inch black-grape Jelly Worm on the first day, was lying next to a bush a short distance from the docks at tournament headquarters. Other fishermen had traveled several miles in search of fish.

"My boat was sitting in 15 to 20 feet of water, and I was throwing the worm to an eight- or nine-foot shelf," said Junior. "Trees had grown up on a sunken island and were barely showing. My partner was fishing too close to me, and I killed five minutes before I could cast to a bush where I thought a big fish would be.

"On my first cast to that bush, the big bass took the worm and headed for 100 feet of water. I'm certain the worm never hit the bottom. I never felt much of a hit but felt something heavy on my line and saw it go off. I tightened up, jumped up clean off the bow of my boat and put everything I had into it. It went into deep water, and I said to myself, 'Go, go, go.' "

Seconds later the bass jumped and shook her huge head, and the Georgian's partner shouted, "Lord, what a bass!"

Junior said, "This bass was very strong. She jumped one more time and made five runs under the boat, stripping line all the time. My partner said, 'I wish I'd brought my big net,' and I told him not to worry."

In a moment the fish was hanging halfway in the net and was quickly put into the boat.

Junior catches most of his bass on points, next to banks, and in back ends of coves. Although he is quite skilled in fishing with the plastic worms, he probably derives even more satisfaction from outwitting a black bass with a wooden or hard plastic imitation of a baitfish.

He agrees with Fred Young of Tennessee, who carved the famous Big-O plug, that it's best to cast a crankbait with a spinning reel. Long and accurate casts can be made with a spinning reel, but even more importantly, while an angler turns the reel handle with his left hand, he sometimes may unconsciously move his right hand slightly in an up-and-down, steady rhythm, thereby twitching the rod tip and giving the swimming bait additional action. If you have any doubts, just watch the spinning rod's tip as a lure is being retrieved; the downward turn of the reel handle perhaps is the key.

In recent years Junior has enjoyed a great amount of success casting the Cordell Hot Spots, the deep-diving, long-lipped Rebels, Jim Bagley's balsa Small Fry series of baitfish imitations, and the deep-running Hellbenders.

He has boated numerous bass in the five- to eight-pound class and three going over nine pounds each that struck the Hot Spot in Lakes Sinclair, Jackson, and Clarks Hill. On West Point Lake he used a Bagley Baby Bass to catch a 9 lb. 5 oz. bass. His biggest bass ever was a 10-pound beauty that hit a jig and plastic frog lure in Georgia's Lake Jackson.

"I'm looking for a hard bottom in the lake when I'm fishing plugs," said Junior. "I like the gravel and rocks and red clay or sand. And, I throw plugs around bushes, stumps, and trees on banks and points.

"I like to throw the Hot Spot around just one lonely stickup and pull it up to it, stop, let it fall three or four inches, and pull it

J. L. "Junior" Collis, a truck driver with an obsession for bass fishing, proudly displays his first 10-pounder. The lunker struck a jig and soft plastic frog bait on the day after Thanksgiving.

on out. I quiver it with the rod a time or two. The bass thinks it's trying to get away, and it makes him hit. Throw the plug six or seven feet beyond a stickup so it won't disturb him or spook him, but it gets his attention. Make three or four casts around it, and if he won't hit, move on."

Many of the crankbaits on the market today have small chambers containing a number of tiny pieces of lead that rattle on the retrieve. Fish obviously hear these unnatural sounds in the water, but it's debatable whether the noise helps the lures attract strikes. One thing is certain, however, the noisy lures definitely will catch fishermen in the stores.

"I used to think it made a difference, and I wouldn't throw a Hot Spot if it didn't rattle," said Junior. "Now I don't think the rattle has anything to do with it. I've caught bass on Spots that don't rattle. The bass sees that Spot moving, and he thinks it's a shad and tries to grab it.

"In the warmer weather, you want to burn it through the water and get 'em excited. In the cold water in winter, you want to slow it down. Shad don't move fast then, and when it gets real cold, they start to die. That's when I let the Spot sink to the bottom and let it dig and stir 'em up. Get it to walkin' on the bottom, it stirs up mud and it excites the fish. They'll hit it on the fall and when it starts up again. Plugs are good in the spring and fall. My four best months are November, December, March, and April. Plugs are real good after the first frost."

Junior favors crankbaits in the threadfin shad, perch, bream, baby bass, and crayfish patterns in natural finishes that look like the real thing. In stained water, he will throw chartreuse, bone, bone-and-orange, black-and-gold, and tiger-colored plugs. His favorite Hot Spot patterns are smoky Joe (black back and gray sides) and "gray bar" (a gray lure with black stripes on sides).

"One day on West Point Lake, I was throwing the Bagley Baby Bass into a big pile of brush you could barely see in that stained water," he said. "I'd throw beyond it, then come back until it hit the brush, let it bounce, stop, and start floating back up. Then I'd crank, and they'd hit it. The bass were on the sides of the brush pile. You'd have to pause. They wouldn't hit it in any other way. We got 15 bass that day up to 8 lb. 14 oz., and my ten biggest weighed 56 pounds. I had four over eight pounds that day."

Junior likes to pull a spinnerbait alongside the trunk of a fallen tree, stopping the retrieve when the bait crosses a limb and allowing it to sink two or three feet with the shiny blade turning. The strike usually comes on the fall, he pointed out, so it's important to be a line-watcher and also to be alert for a sharp tug when the retrieve is resumed.

A Silent Lunker-Hunter

Good fishermen believe that it's almost a sin to make any unnatural sounds in a boat. Take it a step further, and one of the ten commandments of angling is, "Don't make any noise, or you'll spook the fish."

This is especially true in fishing for black bass. My father convinced me that if I dropped the pliers in a wooden or aluminum johnboat, the bass would almost jump out of their skins. If the tackle box were knocked over, the fish would be nervous wrecks, and you had to move the boat a mile down the lake or call it a day and go home.

Dad was a gentle and patient man, and he wouldn't blow his stack when a fishing partner goofed and made a racket in the boat. But, next time he went fishing, Dad invited a much quieter friend to accompany him.

I thought of those lessons in avoiding fish-spooking noise when I met Bill O'Connor of Fort Walton Beach, Florida, who is sort of a living legend in Florida bass angling.

"If a fisherman wants to catch a largemouth bass in the ten-pound class, he absolutely must be as quiet as the proverbial mouse," says O'Connor.

"It's all right to talk, just don't tap any Morse code messages on the side of the boat."

Bill, who works for an airline, fishes for pleasure or competes in national bass tournaments on weekends and vacations. Years ago he learned that the slightest unnatural noise would spook a big fish, and he practices what he preaches, insisting that his fishing partners do the same.

"Most of my bass over ten pounds have been caught without an electric trolling motor running on a boat," he said.

He has caught more than one hundred black bass weighing ten pounds or more. Mounted on walls in his home are his dozen biggest bass, which range from 12 pounds to 15 pounds, 5 ounces. In Florida's Lake Jackson, near Tallahassee, he once fought a bass estimated to weigh 25 pounds, but after a fierce 20-minute battle the huge fish straightened the hooks of a surface plug and escaped. That fish would have exceeded the world record bass' weight of 22 pounds, 4 ounces. The record giant bigmouth was caught in June, 1932, in Georgia's Montgomery Lake, an oxbow pond off the Ocmulgee River near Lumber City.

"I have found that a trolling motor's noise scares a bass weighing over ten pounds when you fish in shallow water," said Bill. "When I guide, I won't fish around trolling motors. You can't even make a long enough cast to get away from it [the motor's sound and vibrations]. I use a sculling paddle and a push-pole in my 14-foot johnboat to go around on a lake.

"Bump the side of a boat, and you scare fish. I carry mats and cover the boat and paddle and everything with them. One scrape on the bottom of a boat will ruin it."

Many of his huge bass have been taken on his homemade soft plastic worm, which has ridges on the back and a flat, beaver-like tail, a lead-weighted hook in the head and a second hook in the center. In his favorite big-bass lakes, he makes the lure imitate a lamprey, an eel-like creature.

"I swim that beaver tail and hump it through the water," he said. "I twitch the rod tip and reel it, and the worm humps and looks more like a lamprey. I fish a worm on top of lily pads and bring it across, then watch 'em bust it like a snake. And I let the worm drop in holes beside the grass, and they nail it."

Bill also catches numerous trophy-size bass on black spoons

with pork rind that he slowly crawls across the bottom; and he has fooled dozens of lunkers with top-water lures.

"I like the Bang-O-Lure and the Nip-i-diddee," he said. "I like light colors on bright days and dark colors on cloudy days, and fish them different ways. I'll let the plug sit on the surface, and I count to 30 sometimes.

"If that doesn't work, I'll twitch it three or four times and stop, and twitch it again. Then I'll fish it fast and churn the water until I find what action the bass want."

The Florida "hawg" hunter likes a rising or falling barometer, particularly during the period just before a front reaches the vicinity of a lake.

"You can fish the day before a front comes through, and you'll tear 'em up," said Bill. "But, after the front passes, and it's a bluebird day, you can go home. I've found that when the moon is full, I will catch more bass early in the morning and late in the evening. But, I catch most of my big bass between 10 A.M. and 2 P.M."

A plastic worm or plastic lizard is much more effective on big bass than a fast-running crankbait because large bass don't want to expend a lot of energy in grabbing a meal.

One day in Lake Jackson, Bill and his partner pulled out 11 bass for a stringer totalling 128 pounds. Several gigantic bass broke 20- and 30-pound monofilament line that day.

"I've found some days you can catch them on purple worms with red tails," he said. "And then they'll quit. You'll have to change to a black worm, and that shade makes a difference.

"I've seen them when they hit a worm that was sitting perfectly still, and other times they'd want it humping in the water like it's swimming. A plastic lizard is almost as good as a worm. One day in the spring I got a 10 lb. 8 oz. bass on a Fliptail lizard."

A bass weighing six to eight pounds usually provides the best fight, except for fertile Lake Jackson's ten-pounders, which are young and strong.

"In most lakes a bass weighing over ten pounds will make two runs and wallow on the surface a time or two, and after that there's not much fight left," he said. "In Florida's Lake Jackson, though, I've seen bass weighing over ten pounds jump out of the water."

When Bill said the biggest bass that he ever released weighed 11 pounds, a fisherman sitting at a table in a fishing camp on Georgia's Lake Sinclair almost choked on iced tea.

It's really astounding that one fisherman could have boated over one hundred bass exceeding ten pounds. I knew a very skilled bass angler in south Georgia who fished 30 years before landing his first ten-pounder. Many fishermen never catch a ten-pounder in an entire lifetime.

On a lovely spring morning several years ago, I had the pleasure of fishing with Bill O'Connor on Lake Juniper, a shallow, stumpy lake near De Funiak Springs in northwest Florida.

He used a push-pole to move the aluminum johnboat slowly along the grassy shoreline, and, with the aid of polarized glasses, he searched for bass beds that had been fanned in the clear, 65-degree water. Vegetation covered the bottom, and bass had made saucer-shaped nests that weren't difficult to spot unless the wind created a lot of ripple on the surface.

Suddenly, he jammed the end of the long push-pole into the sandy bottom to stop the boat. "There's a big bass on a bed, Charles," he said. "She's a monster."

He backed up the little boat and held it against the grass-covered bank, and I cast a black Fliptail plastic lizard just beyond the bed.

"You're just going to feel a little tick when she picks it up out of the bed," said Bill. "Just be ready to set the hook, and hang on. She's really a monster."

Sure enough, moments later I felt a slight tick, about the way it would feel if a honeybee had collided with the monofilament line. The line jumped when the bass picked up the soft plastic bait to remove it from the nest, undoubtedly, feeling that the "lizard" was a threat to her precious eggs.

I set the hook and held the fiberglass rod high, and my arms quivered in response to the giant fish's astounding amount of power as she streaked out of the nest. The bass swam about 20 feet to my left before she made an explosive jump, leaving a big hole in the surface as she strained to get her extremely thick body out of the water.

I gasped, unable to believe my eyes, when she violently shook her massive head with her giant mouth wide open and threw the lizard into the air. The humongous bass crashed back to the surface, sending a pretty good-size wave toward our boat, and swam away as free as a bird.

I bent over, staring at my tackle box, shaking my head in frustration, then turned to Bill and asked, "How big do you reckon that fish is?"

Bill appeared to be nearly as shaken as I, and he replied, "That was the biggest bass I've ever seen. She was undoubtedly the biggest I've seen anywhere. That fish would have weighed 20 pounds."

The bass would have topped the Florida state record by one pound. I gulped and felt even worse.

"I believe you should have set the hook twice, maybe three times," said Bill. "The hook must have been in the hard part of her mouth, and the barb didn't penetrate. You just can't set a hook too hard on a big bass."

A few minutes later, Bill slowly dragged a black plastic lizard into a bass's bed, and I watched him set the hook with terrific force. Then he jerked the rod up hard two more times to make certain the bass was securely hooked.

The big bass leaped out of the water three times, a rather surprising feat considering her size, and stripped off several feet of 20-pound test line, although Bill had tightened the baitcasting reel's drag with his pliers.

I grabbed the landing net, held it over the side and waited for him to lead the handsome "hawg" into it. She was really a beauty, tipping the scales at 11 lb. 12 oz.

The fish was mighty strong to be able to take line on the runs.

I checked the reel's drag, and I couldn't make the line slip off the spool without risking cutting my fingers.

Top-Water Bassin' Evangelist

Relatively few anglers cast top-water lures for black bass in their favorite lakes and rivers in the South nowadays. Some of them bait their hooks with shiners, lizards, or nightcrawlers. Many others spend long hours dragging soft plastic worms across the bottom or retrieving diving, vibrating crankbaits.

Calvin "Cal" Jaynes of Conyers, Georgia, observed this trend away from surface fishing and described it as an enigma.

"I cannot conceive that anybody couldn't get totally carried away with top-water fishing," he said. "My experience over the years has been that when I have had an opportunity to take somebody out and really introduce him to some honest-to-goodness top-water fishing, where the bass just blow a hole in the surface, you make a confirmed believer out of him. I don't have any problem, and he wonders why he didn't do it many years ago."

A native of Detroit who works for an insurance company in Atlanta, Jaynes became a serious bass angler in 1946, while attending Bryan College in Dayton, Tennessee, on the banks of Lake Chicamauga.

"I got married, and we had a mobile home 200 feet from the lake," he said. "I got a mountaineer to make me a bateau with ten dollars worth of lumber and ten dollars worth of labor. I put some caulking between the planks and sealed it up, and I'd run there morning and evening and do a little fishing."

Jaynes, unlike so many of the modern-day fishermen, measures the success of a day's fishing in terms of quality, not quantity.

"I think Jack Wingate, operator of a Lake Seminole fishing camp put it pretty succinctly," he said. "The joy was in the fishing, and catching the fish was the icing on the cake."

He believes that fishing is a great escape from the problems, tensions, and pressures of city life.

Years ago he concluded that the black bass is the greatest freshwater game fish because he is, by nature, a mean critter that viciously strikes a lure and a ferocious fighter that can nearly pull a rod and reel out of a person's hands. And watching the bass's dazzling display of acrobatics is a truly unforgettable experience.

"I love to see him jump," said Jaynes. "In the moonlight when they're hitting top water and you see that big, old white belly come up and stand up there and throw water, I don't think there's anything in the world that compares with it."

During the past 30 years, Jaynes has used dozens of surface lures, but he now sticks with six favorites—the Creek Chub Darter, Heddon Chugger Spook, Rapala, Rebel, Heddon Lucky 13, and black Jitterbug.

"The crux of the whole thing is the action that you give to the lure," he said. "Give the maximum amount of agitation with the minimum amount of forward motion of the lure.

"What I'm trying to do is simulate, as best I can, an injured or dying fish which certainly doesn't move like a jet. I want to make it an easy target for an old fat bass that doesn't want to chase it all over the lake."

Many fishermen make the mistake of working a top-water lure too fast and too far with twitches of their rods.

"The key to the thing is to imitate a dying fish or bird or mouse or something, and if you move it too fast and rush it through the water, they're not going after it unless they are suicide bent."

Deep, clear, 38,000-acre Lake Sidney Lanier, less than an

hour's drive north of Atlanta, is his favorite bass lake, and in the spring and early summer he casts for largemouths beginning at sunrise and again for a couple of hours before sundown.

"Clear water doesn't affect top-water fishing at all," Jaynes said. "They are hitting at a silhouette, and this is the reason that color isn't significant. When the sun is shining, all they see is a silhouette. I think they'll hit on top in clear water when they wouldn't dream of hitting many underwater lures where they get a three-dimensional view of the lure, and it actually has some color. I deliberately look for clear water."

During the spring and early summer, Jaynes looks for weed beds, tree tops, logs, boat docks, boat houses, and other areas that provide shade in which the fish can hide.

"I found, for instance, on Lake Rabun [in the northeast Georgia mountains], which is very deep, very clear and has very little cover, the boat houses and the trees were consistently the best place to catch bass," he said. And, he added, "Some of the trees were down so deep you couldn't see them. When a fish came up in mid-day in July and August when it was so hot you'd just broil in the sun, they'd come from down so far they'd completely clear the water on the strike and turn cartwheels."

Jaynes attracts the attention of black bass with a surface plug in somewhat the same fashion that a burlesque dancer captivates her audience. He keeps the lure moving and drives them nearly out of their minds.

If a fisherman gets a sizable percentage of his strikes more than ten feet from where he thought the bass ought to be, such as a tree top, he's playing his artificial bait right.

"This means they followed it out and decided it was what they wanted," he explained. "If the only strikes were right where you thought the fish was, they are more likely to be impulse strikes. You know you really are in business when the fish made a calculated decision to hit the lure. You gave him an opportunity to follow it into open water where there is no obstacle to obstruct his view."

If a person holds the fishing rod vertically while working the lure, there is a bow in the line that takes away some of the bait's action.

"I hold the rod at a 45-degree angle, move it toward the lure, pick up half a turn—nine inches on my baitcasting reel, and in the same motion, without hesitation, bring it back.

"What I'm doing, I've picked up nine inches, and now I pop the lure nine inches forward, and, instantly, I move the rod back toward the lure. And, I've picked up the next nine inches."

Jaynes favors a five-foot, stiff baitcasting rod and 17- to 20-pound monofilament line. For years he fished with a fiberglass rod, then he discovered a graphite rod was much lighter and more sensitive. Recently, he bought a five-foot boron rod, which he now believes may be the ultimate top-water stick. It's lightweight, very sensitive, and has perhaps greater strength than the graphite or glass.

He explained how he works a plug around the target area where he thinks a bass may be lying in ambush for baitfish.

"If it is a solitary stump or tree limb or target with water behind it, I prefer to throw about five feet to the other side," said Jaynes. "Start the lure back rather than let it smack on top of them. On the other hand, if it's inside of a tree partially in the water and partially out, and you have a wedge to throw into, you have no choice. But I prefer to let the lure fall onto the water instead of driving it in there with a low trajectory and letting it smash and tumble. I don't think that gets the fish."

If a bass is in the area and wants to hit a crippled minnow, the odds are very high that he will strike on your first cast.

The biggest bass that Jaynes has caught on a top-water plug weighed 9 lb. 8 oz., and he has boated dozens of others in the lunker class soon after sunrise and shortly before dark on Georgia lakes.

One rainy day on Lake Hartwell, Jaynes and his partner caught and released 100 bass between 6 A.M. and 1 P.M.

"If I decided to throw to a log that is in line with me, I would fish the entire length of the log," he said. "If it was crosswise and more than 12 feet long, I'd make two casts, one at each end.

It depends on the mood the bass are in. Sometimes they won't move more than a foot to hit your lure. Other times they will move nearly 20 feet."

He strongly disagrees with fishermen who say that a bass "missed" a plug on a surface strike.

Jaynes smiled and said, "He never misses when he wants it. When people say a bass missed the lure, he didn't miss it. He did precisely what he wanted to do—drive away the fish that didn't belong in his territory."

On the shaded sides of boat houses, Jaynes gets a lot of surface strikes as he makes his lure dance toward deeper water. In the spring and summer, he also looks for weed beds in which bass lurk and baitfish try to hide from predators.

One day in late March, Jaynes walked into the bait shop and cafe at Jack Wingate's Lunker Lodge on Seminole, and found the owner dozing in a big, soft chair behind the counter. Jaynes tried to keep a straight face and remarked in a serious tone, "Jack, you told me a lie."

Wingate was puzzled. He rubbed sleep from his eyes and asked, "What was that?"

Jaynes said, "You told me there were ten-pound bass in that area."

"There weren't any ten-pounders?" asked Wingate.

"Nope," said Jaynes, no longer able to suppress a grin, "just 9¼-pounders."

Both men laughed, and Wingate reached for his camera. The Conyers angler had ribbed his old friend for two days about not sending him to an area of Seminole where trophy-size bass were hungry.

By that Saturday, March 22, the very heavy rainfall in Georgia had caused the Flint River, which flows into Seminole, to reach its highest level since 1929. The Chattahoochee River also was far beyond its banks. Even Spring Creek, normally gin-clear, had become heavily stained, nearly as bad as the rivers.

That morning the wind caused a little chop on the water, and there was cloud cover—ideal conditions for surface lures. So,

Wingate suggested that Jaynes might find a ten-pounder in a shallow, timber-lined area just off the main part of the reservoir.

Jaynes kept his faith even after hearing a local fellow remark in the cafe, "They ain't gonna hit when the river is runnin' that high."

He tied on a five-inch, cigar-shaped Rebel in the black-and-silver pattern, a bait that resembles a crippled fish when the rod tip is twitched in his familiar, rhythmic fashion.

"We were fishing in a sink hole that had big dead trees in it," Jaynes told me. "An alligator would come up once in a while. We guessed it was eight feet long. We had picked up some bass, but they were hitting it with their mouths closed sometimes, driving the lure off the beds. One of those fish must have come two feet out of the water when he hit that thing and just bounced it into the air."

A big fish suddenly swirled in about four feet of water close to the timber, and Jaynes spotted the action out of the corner of his eye, then switched on the bow-mounted electric trolling motor to maneuver his 16-foot bass boat into position for a cast.

"I threw it right in where he'd been, and I just moved it twice," said Jaynes. "He just blew a hole in that lake that looked like it was three feet across. The bass really nailed it.

"The fighting bass put on quite a show, running under the boat, then breaking water and wallowing twice before stripping off more of the 20-pound monofilament line from the freespool baitcasting reel."

Within spitting distance were trees and logs against which the fish easily could have cut the line as if it had been sewing thread. You can understand why Calvin keeps strong monofilament line on his reel after seeing Seminole's millions of stumps.

In a few moments, Jaynes wore the fish to a frazzle, pulled it to the side of his boat, and reached for a well-earned trophy, a 9 lb. 4 oz. largemouth bass.

"There were just a few eggs left," Jaynes said. "The bass had a flat belly, and she'd already spawned. Jack thought she would have weighed another pound and a half carrying the eggs. I figured the bass would have weighed at least ten pounds before spawning."

Big Plugs, Big Fish

The alarm had awakened Randy Mayberry before dawn that spring morning in Sandersville, Georgia. The University of Georgia business major had intended to make his first cast in the farm pond at what country folks call "first light."

Unfortunately, his old car broke down, and 45 minutes passed before he could push his johnboat away from the bank. Setting his 6 ft. 4 in., 190-pound frame as comfortably as possible in the little aluminum boat, he started the stern-mounted electric trolling motor and crept within casting range of a brushy tree top in 12 to 15 feet of water.

"I cast a frog-colored Creek Chub Injured Minnow beyond the tree," said Randy. "The fish was lying under that brush. As soon as the lure passed him, the seven-pound bass nailed it."

Several minutes later, the Injured Minnow aroused the appetite or anger of an 8 lb. 14 oz. bass beside another tree top in the 35-acre, fertilized lake, which has been stocked with bass, bluegills, shellcrackers, and catfish for over 20 years.

Randy's wife, a schoolteacher who understands fishing fever, says, "He'll always wonder what else he might have hooked if the car hadn't conked out that morning."

Randy became interested in fishing when he was 13 years old and began casting with his grandfather's old spin-cast reel. A week later he owned his first reel.

"I still fish a lot with plastic worms when the weather is hot and the bass are deeper, but I'd rather catch a bass on a top-water plug than any other way," he said. "It's more exciting to see the bass smash a plug on the surface."

In the same week that he boated the two lunkers in less than an hour, Randy also pulled a nine-pounder out of the farm lake.

He fishes with a free-spool baitcasting reel, a stiff 5- or 5½-foot fiberglass rod, and 17- to 25-pound monofilament line. His favorite surface plugs are the Injured Minnow, Dalton Special, Creek Chub Plunker, and Creek Chub jointed Darter in the perch or frog finish.

"I've always liked the larger-size plugs," he said. "I've thought a smaller plug would get you smaller fish."

The mood of the fish in that particular hour determines the speed that he works his imitation of an injured baitfish.

"Generally, I'll just throw 10 or 15 feet on the other side of a tree or log and pop it loud at first at a fairly fast retrieve," said Randy. "Then when I get the plug right by the tree, I'll slow it down almost to a crawl. If he doesn't hit it then, I'll bring it back in fast. Sometimes I get a strike on the way back, nearer the boat. Usually, if the bass is going to strike, he will hit it on the first cast."

He added, "If that doesn't work, I'll throw the plug to the other side of the structure, reel it fast and stop it right there by the tree and wait 30 seconds. Then I might make one more cast."

Although many of his bass are caught along shallow banks at dawn or near sundown, Randy usually hooks his bigger fish close to trees standing in water 8 to 15 or 18 feet deep.

"I've caught good-size bass lying around trees in deeper water when the sun is high in the sky," he said. "I know a cloudy day is best, but you'd be surprised at the way they'll strike a surface plug in deeper water on a bright day in the spring."

This lake has yielded a largemouth bass weighing almost 12 pounds, and Randy feels confident a 14- to 16-pounder is lying next to one of those trees waiting to inhale a careless bream.

"I'm going to start trying them at night in the summer with a surface plug and a black worm," he said.

III
Trout

Ben Newcomer casts a dry fly for trout in a river that is only a few minutes' drive from his home. (Photo—George Clark.)

Casting Close to Home

An Atlanta fisherman, observing with dismay the terribly high gasoline prices, is thankful that his favorite fishing hole is just 30 minutes from home. Ben Newcomer, 70, a retired businessman, catches a number of different species of game fish and pan fish in the Chattahoochee River in metropolitan Atlanta.

"I've fished for trout with varying degrees of success in the Greybull River drainage of Wyoming, the Yellow Breeches Creek in Pennsylvania, the Oconalufey River in North Carolina, the Little Tennessee River in Tennessee, and lesser known trout waters too numerous to mention," he said. "The cost of these expeditions in time and money? Plenty. Just ask my wife, Lillian, who attempts to keep the budget straight at our house. On second thought, please don't ask her. Things are peaceful at home right now."

On a typical summer afternoon, Newcomer goes fishing in the Chattahoochee River, and he lands his limit of brown and rainbow trout, which are 12 to 14 inches long, and releases two smaller fish.

"Of course, you should have seen the one that got away," he said, and I could imagine a rainbow nearly as long as his arm. "Contrasting this trip with the ones mentioned, I was wading the Chattahoochee above Holcombe Bridge just 30 minutes after leaving my driveway. Also, for this day and time, these are good fish in anybody's trout stream. Not trophies by any means, but still respectable."

The low cost of his fishing trip was very impressive.

"The costs of today's expedition?" he said. "About a gallon of gasoline, one bottom-snagged, ⅛-ounce, gold-bladed spinner, and about five hours of fishing time. Now, somewhere in this tale there should be a moral for Atlanta trout fishermen, if I could just think what it is. I'll bet Lillian could spot it in a minute."

Newcomer, a native of Cody, Wyoming, offered me some advice that I'll try to remember on my next fishing trip. "When you're ready to call it a day after fishing for hours on a river or lake, make one last cast, and you might hook a trophy."

A beautiful, 18-inch rainbow trout hanging on his den wall struck a white Shyster spinning lure during snow flurries on the Chattahoochee River below the Morgan Falls dam in December, 1967. It was a last-cast fish. Displayed next to it is a handsome, hook-jawed brown trout that Newcomer landed after making "a half-hearted, last-ditch, upstream cast" with a brown Rooster Tail spinner on Georgia's Soque River in October, 1971.

While Newcomer was trying out his "latest budget-wrecker," an 8½-foot graphite fly rod, he scored again with his famous last cast. He had waded 100 yards in the Chattahoochee River below Georgia 20, hooking two little rainbows and then losing his last Montana Nymph on a snag. His faith a bit dampened, he walked to the river bank, filled his pipe with tobacco, and figured it was time to return home.

"Then, about 40 feet out in the current, something dimpled the surface," he said. "Hastily tying on a No. 10 brown Woolly Worm, I got off one of the few good casts of the day, with the fly landing several feet above where the fish had risen. As it floated down in the surface film, I gave it one small twitch, and a big brown trout engulfed it like a cat pouncing on an unwary mouse.

"With a 3½-pound test tippet on my leader, he could obviously not be horsed in. After some 15 cardiac-arresting-type minutes and several reel-screeching runs, he finally came to the net. He turned out to be a fine 18-inch, 3-pound specimen of *salmo trutta*."

Newcomer said the brown trout was attracted by the Woolly Worm because it had been feeding upon drowned wasps and large beetles.

An Unforgettable Battle

E. L. "Roy" Fincher of Riverdale, Georgia, a bakery foreman, agrees with Newcomer that the Chattahoochee in metropolitan Atlanta offers outstanding fishing for trout. One Saturday afternoon he spent 41 of the most exciting and suspenseful minutes of his life fighting a 14 lb. 3 oz. brown trout. His trophy was 28½ inches long and had a 20-inch girth.

The Georgia state record brown trout weighed 18 lbs. 2 oz., and was caught by William M. Lowery in Rock Creek on May 6, 1967.

Fincher and his fishing partner, Alan Davidson, also took eight rainbow trout between 10 and 14 inches while fishing from a 17-foot canoe between Old Jones bridge and Holcombe Bridge on the Chattahoochee, just north of Doraville.

The Riverdale fisherman baited his short-shanked No. 8 hook with a cricket and fished with an ultra-light spinning reel and rod and six-pound test monofilament line. He pinched three BB shots onto the line 18 inches above the hook.

"I didn't use a cork, and I fished on the bottom, trying for a natural presentation of the bait," said Fincher. "The water was greenish, a little off-color, and the wind was blowing the canoe around on the river."

They dropped the anchor, not realizing it immediately lodged in rocks, and began casting from midstream into holes six to eight feet deep. Fincher had pulled a 5 lb. 12 oz. brown trout out of that area in the previous summer.

"When that big brown trout struck, it felt like a locomotive wide open, and the drag on my reel was screaming," he said. "It took about 75 yards of line down the river before I turned it. At first I thought it might weigh six or eight pounds, then it just ran away with it, and I stood up in the canoe. The anchor was lodged in a rock, and we couldn't go after the trout."

Several times Fincher managed to gain a few yards of line, but the trout sped downstream or across the river again.

"After 20 minutes, I got the trout up to the boat, and when he saw it, he took off again," he said. "There was no use trying to challenge it."

He yelled to a couple of nearby anglers who were watching the battle, Warner Bonner and John Arndt, hoping they had a big landing net. They didn't, and Fincher's little net would have to do the job.

"I hooked that fish at 2:35 P.M., and the fight lasted 41 minutes," said Fincher. "The trout must have made ten to fifteen runs. I was shook up, and had to swap hands with that rod because I was beginning to have trouble with blood circulation."

The brown trout rolled on the surface, slapping the water with its big tail and sending spray ten feet across the surface.

"I finally was able to pull the fish to the side of our canoe," said Fincher. "Alan reached with the net, and I grabbed the trout's lip."

Bonner said, "You should have seen how his hand was bleeding. But, he didn't feel a thing. He was so excited. I told my fishing partner that if Roy Fincher fought that trout until midnight, we'd be sitting right here. I believe Roy is the best trout fisherman in Georgia."

He added, "Really, that fight with the brown trout was the most exciting thing I've seen in sports since I watched the Olympics on television."

Bonner, who had watched in amazement as Fincher stood up and kept his balance in a white-water canoe that has no keel, said, "I saw him change hands with the spinning rod and shake the hand that was cramping, trying to get circulation back in it. Near the end, both hands were hurting him."

The Secret—Natural Movement

W. A. (Bill) Sims III of Atlanta is another angler who discovered that one of America's finest trout streams was virtually in his own backyard. He and his wife were rafting down the Chattahoochee River below the Morgan Falls dam. He had brought along a spinning rod and reel but didn't realize so many trout were in the river. He began casting a spinning lure and within a short time caught his limit of brown trout.

Since then he has spent hundreds of hours casting artificial lures or live bait from the bank or a boat or while wading with a tube. The marvelous trout fishery has provided him with many memorable moments in angling, but he also points out the tranquility and beauty of that river have been good food for the soul.

In the summer the surface temperature of the Chattahoochee in metropolitan Atlanta usually remains in the 60s, rising to 70 degrees only briefly at the peak of heat waves. The water is quite cool because it is discharged through turbines at the bottom of the Lake Lanier dam and, therefore, is very favorable downstream for trout habitat. Trout normally cannot tolerate water which is warmer than 70 degrees or that is too low in dissolved oxygen.

Sims was proud of a 5 lb. 4 oz. brown trout that was 24 inches long, a beauty he hooked in the Chattahoochee, and he has boated numerous browns in the 16- to 18-inch class.

Sims recommends that fishermen release small trout to give them an opportunity to increase their weight and length for the next season.

"If fishermen would release those small trout, the river would have lots of big browns," he said. "I have seen people walk out with their limits of nine- and ten-inch trout. It just kills my soul to see them keep such small trout. I don't keep trout smaller than twelve inches."

Sims fishes with an ultra-light spinning reel, four-pound test line, and a graphite rod.

He baits a No. 6 hook with crickets and pinches a BB-size lead on the line 18 inches above. His favorite artificial lures are the small Mepps spinners and Rooster Tails with gold blades.

"You want to float the cricket as naturally as you can," he said. "The secret is natural movement. The water will carry the cricket to where the trout are lying. You can't second-guess them, whether they are behind an eddy or lying in a pool. The fish will be where the food washes up."

He sets the hook with a slight jerk of the wrist, and the sharp point of a No. 6 hook easily penetrates most areas of the fish's mouth.

"You want the river to be low so you can wade," he said. "Anytime just prior to a weather front's passage through is always good, provided the river is not high. I fished in the river one day when the air temperature never rose above 32 degrees, and I got my limit of trout."

The river offers brown trout an abundant supply of food, enabling them to grow more rapidly than they would in mountain streams. They feed on threadfin shad that come from Lake Lanier, baby bream, numerous insects and their larva, crayfish, lizards, and also worms that rain washes into the stream.

Sims, like Ben Newcomer, observed that the Chattahoochee just north of Atlanta is the home of numerous species of fish. He has caught not only brown trout and rainbows, but also largemouth bass, a two-pound smallmouth bass, bluegills, redbreast, chain pickerel (jackfish), crappie, and carp.

Natives Offer a Challenge

In the little north Georgia mountain town of Ellijay, Bill Green assured me that the good Lord created lots of mighty fine fish for us folks on earth to catch, but none can match the majestic beauty, quality as a fighter, or the acrobatics of the rainbow trout. Green has enjoyed fishing for trout over 30 years in the picturesque mountain streams near his home.

"It's a beautiful fish, a great game fish," he said. "I like to catch the native trout. They come up out of the water and walk the water. They'll fan at you jumping. It's really a thrill to see him jump in the air and try to shake that hook out of his mouth."

Green fishes with a Zebco 33 closed-face reel, ten-pound test line, a medium action 5½-foot rod, and a No. 8 hook. A split shot is pinched onto the line just above a swivel on his leader.

"You don't have to have expensive equipment to catch fish, but you've got to know how to catch them," he said. "You have to find the trout, know their habits, know how to wade the stream. It's a challenge to me to get out and catch a good trout. Fishing is good medicine. It's about the best medicine a fellow can take. You can forget your worries and relax."

On a wall in his home hang a 20-inch rainbow trout and a 25-inch brown trout.

"I'd rather catch one native rainbow trout than 50 bass," said Green, laughing. "I'm partial to trout fishing. My favorite bait is a nightcrawler. I use a flashlight with a cover to dim the light and go to a friend's backyard after a rain and crawl around on the ground and look for nightcrawlers."

A person must know which end of the worm to grab, or the long, fat bait will spring back and race into a hole. The nightcrawlers have a knack of hanging onto a little hole in the ground.

Green said he would "guarantee" that a No. 8 hook would hold any fish in his favorite creeks. On the previous Saturday, he fished at a friend's place on a stream and landed six native rainbows measuring from 12 to 15 inches.

"A native rainbow trout is a wilder fish than a stocked trout and gives you a real fight," he said. "And, it's more wary. If you hang him one time and lose him, then he won't bite again for a day or two. A stocked trout usually keeps on hitting the bait."

His best one-day catch in recent years included eight rainbows that went into the frying pan and fifteen that he released in the mountain stream.

On a typical day, he walks two or three miles in chest-high waders and felt-bottom shoes in a cool, clear creek or river. Green, who admits he falls once in a while, said, "Everybody can't go out and wade streams. I can tell a fellow who has rainbow fished before and knows what it's all about. You can tell by the way he handles himself in the water."

The 4 lb. 8 oz. brown trout that a taxidermist mounted was caught by Green with a nightcrawler in a three-foot-deep, very clear, small stream.

"Notice the big head and mouth on that German brown," said Green. "That was an old fish, but the small stream didn't have enough food for the body to develop more. Look at those teeth in his mouth.

"I was standing in that creek when the fish came swimming upstream and came by me. I didn't even know it was around. It sort of scared me because it was so big. I thought it was an alligator."

He was kidding, of course. Gators don't live in the mountain streams, but that German brown pulled as hard as one.

Trophies Galore

The sun was shining on a glorious day in the north Georgia mountains, but few rays found their way between leaves of the lush green forest bordering Waters Creek near the community of Turner's Corner.

A deer stood on the shaded bank of a trophy trout stream and curiously watched three men cautiously approach a pool, perhaps wondering why these creatures weren't holding the long sticks that weekend visitors bring. Allen Padgett, manager of the Georgia Game and Fish Division's Chestatee Wildlife Management Area, 14 miles north of Cleveland, reached into a bucket and threw a handful of pellets of trout chow into the creek.

Suddenly the quiet, deep pool became alive with the kind of rainbow trout and brook trout that people dream of hooking.

The slurp, slap, and slosh of handsome trout rolling and boiling on the surface, seizing the familiar pellets that are served every other day, made goose bumps rise on my arms, and I wished I could hook such fish on ultra-light spinning tackle.

But it would have to be on a Saturday or Sunday, the only two days the trophy trout stream was open to the public. A fishing permit can be bought at the checking station next to Padgett's house on Dicks Creek.

Waters Creek yielded a Georgia state record brook trout weighing 5 lb. 5 oz., caught by James Harper of Austell on September 3, 1973.

Padgett has seen a rainbow trout that is probably the biggest in the whole creek, but he hastens to add that it is also one of the smartest or spookiest fish, too.

"There is one granddaddy in the creek, a hoss of a rainbow, that will go 30-something inches," said Padgett. "It would weigh eight to ten pounds, a monster. I have seen him twice. No, I haven't named that fish."

In order to qualify as a keeper, a rainbow trout or a brown trout must be at least 22 inches long, and the minimum size for brook trout is 18 inches.

"This is an artificial lure-only type of stream," said Padgett. "You can't use corn, worms, crickets, salmon eggs. You must fish with a single barbless hook, No. 6 or smaller, and the landing net must be less than two feet long. And, you are allowed to keep just one fish. Remember, if you fish with spinning lures, like Mepps and Rooster Tails, you've got to cut off all except one hook."

In Boggs Creek and Dicks Creek on this 24,000-acre wildlife management area, the stocked trout generally run three to a pound.

Padgett smiled and explained, "In Waters Creek, the frustrating part is that these fish are stream grown. They are not dumb hatchery fish. They are stream savvy. By the time a trout gets keeper-size, he has been caught innumerable times. They are fed a trout chow pelleted food every other day. So far this year they have caught 12 keeping-size fish."

At the checking station, Padgett has seen some keeper-size rainbows or brookies with ten to fifteen hook scars in their mouths.

I wondered whether an artificial bait that resembled trout chow pellets would be a productive bait.

Padgett chuckled and said, "Yes, a lure in the shape of the pellet works. That's sort of like matching the hatch. Some people don't realize this. You cut a piece of cork and put a No. 10 hook in it. But it still ain't easy. A 22-inch trout is no laughing matter. Even if you hang him in this creek, it's snagged up a lot and tight. A 22-inch rainbow in this stream is going to put up one heckuva fight."

Padgett said that a popular spinning lure has become so familiar to trout in Waters Creek that they fear the bait and run away from it.

He said, "I don't believe they have caught keepers on a spinning lure this year. They have caught some keepers on bass plugs and plastic worms. Right now the brown Fliptail plastic worm is good.

"You throw those trout something they have not seen before, and you are liable to come out of there with a keeper trout. There have been several fly rods broken on Waters Creek by big trout."

Dedication Required

Steve Johnson, a member of the Atlanta Police Bureau's SWAT team, has learned to expect the unexpected, even when he goes fishing. He has been accustomed to catching trout in Georgia mountain streams in the spring and summer, when the weather is warm and beautiful.

The scene is familiar to hundreds of fishermen who like to try to outsmart the shy rainbows in a cool stream that belongs in a photo on a calendar. Flowers are in bloom, birds are singing, the good Lord has painted the mountains completely green again, and it's almost time to have a picnic on the bank. If you could make "lines" rhyme, you'd write a poem about this wonderful sport of fishing.

Johnson described an entirely different fishing scene, convincing me a dedicated trout angler will endure as much punishment in the outdoors in February as a spoon-jigging, numb-with-cold bass angler on Georgia's Lake Sidney Lanier.

Johnson and his wife, also an ardent angler, heard about the winter trout season in a section of North Carolina, and they drove to Cherokee to try their luck in the Oconalufey River.

On that mid-February day, he was walking on the bank and casting a 1/16-ounce black Rooster Tail with a gold blade on an ultra-light spinning reel and rod with six-pound line. He remembered that in the same area the previous spring, a handsome trout had grabbed the same kind of spinning lure but had gotten away.

"That fish had wrapped the line around my wife's boots as we waded in the river, and the line broke," said Johnson. "Well, in February it was cold up there, and it was snowing on us by five o'clock. In that clear water, I had seen one trout—looked like it would have gone three pounds—make a pass at my lure. Three casts later, I slowed down my retrieve in that cold water, and the nice brown trout struck."

As snow flakes continued to fall, the shivering policeman watched a 5 lb. 12 oz. brown trout leap from a deep pool near rocks and shake its head, "like it was in slow motion," trying to throw the lure.

Dashing downstream in the river and stripping line off the spinning reel, the trout jumped two more times, giving an exhibition of acrobatics that would have looked great on film.

"I had a big dip net with me, and I finally was able to net the trout, and the hook came out of his mouth," said Johnson.

"The next day was Sunday, and we got up early and started casting again. The weather was even colder. The blade on the Rooster Tail froze and wouldn't turn when I pulled it out of the water to cast again. I tried to blow my breath on it and thaw it out. The monofilament line was getting stiff, too, and ice formed on the spinning rod's line guides. It was just impossible to do any more fishing."

Johnson said a trout puts up a very strong fight in a river in the winter, but it was quite curious to observe the jumps that reminded him of a slow-motion movie. He recommended that an angler retrieve a lure much more slowly in the winter than in the spring and summer.

"In the spring and summer, I fish the Chattahoochee close to Atlanta and also make a trip up to Cherokee," he said. "I've had my best luck on the Rooster Tail, the yellow coachdog pattern and, also, the solid black with a gold blade. If you want to catch big trout, you'll do better with artificial lures than live bait, I believe. I caught an 18-inch rainbow in a stream near Cherokee, and I had mounted a 24-inch rainbow that weighed 6 lb. 12 oz., that I caught on a frog-colored Bomber in Lake Lanier."

In one day in 1966, on Lake Lanier, Johnson landed three rainbows that weighed over five pounds each. His wife pulled an 18-inch rainbow trout out of the Oconalufey River the same day the previous spring that he lost a beautiful brown trout.

An Inexpensive Catch

Sometimes we are reminded by youngsters that big fish can be hooked without spending a lot of money on fishing tackle and lures. A good example occurred in June, 1969, when a 12-year-old Lithonia boy, Barry Lowe, fishing with a fly that cost a few pennies in a country store, caught what then was a Georgia state record 3 lb. 12 oz. brook trout in Moccasin Creek.

Leon Kirkland, who then was chief of fisheries, remarked, "This would be a big brook trout anywhere in the United States. We are really tickled to see a bigger state record. It makes Georgia's trout fishing look even better in the eyes of fishermen in other states."

A few years later, the record was broken when James Harper pulled a 5 lb. 5 oz. beauty out of Waters Creek.

Barry said, "The fly was bought in a country store, and I think you got about ten for a dollar. It looks like a bumble bee and is yellow with black stripes."

The boy, fishing with a closed-face reel, tied the fly on ten-pound test monofilament line, dropped the bait into Moccasin Creek and watched it float downstream.

"The fish hit it," said Barry. "I saw it go into his mouth. I just jerked up the rod. He had just stayed there wiggling his tail, but then he ran. I didn't try to play him, because he might have run under a rock. He came out of the water about four times, and I pulled him up on the bank."

Barry and his cousin, David Lowe, 11, ran back to the campsite, where the proud angler informed his parents, Mr. and Mrs. H. Stewart Lowe of Lithonia, "Boy, that is big enough for our supper." Barry's uncle, Charlie Lowe, obviously impressed, told him, "That's a record fish."

Double Strikes

In 30 years of serious fishing for trout, John W. Timmons of Atlanta had never seen anything like it. He can still hardly believe that the unusual action had occurred in only a 30-minute period.

In April, 1971, Timmons asked his son, John W. Timmons, Jr., a captain in the Marines who was soon to leave for Okinawa, to try his luck for rainbows in some beautiful shoals near Jones Bridge on the Chattahoochee River just north of Atlanta.

"We started wading in the river about seven-fifteen that morning," said Timmons. "I was fly fishing with two wet flies, one with brown hackle and the other with gray, using both at the same time. I've never seen anything to beat it. I got three double strikes in only 30 minutes, and I landed all six of the trout. They were not very large—about ten inches each—but they put up a good fight."

John, Jr. gave up on the flies and started fishing with kernels of corn and landed half a dozen rainbows.

"Before this, I had had only two double strikes in 30 years," said Timmons. "Once in the summer of 1970, it happened, and another time eight or ten years earlier.

"When I had that double strike in the summer of 1970, they must have struck simultaneously. It felt like only one strike, and I figured I had a whopper. One went 12½ inches, the other 10½ inches. But this time I could see one trout strike and then the other one hit. It was really uncanny."

On the opening day of trout season in 1941, Timmons picked up some valuable fishing tips from a man named Rosser who was project superintendent at a CCC camp at Smoke Mont, North Carolina.

"I had never fished for trout, so I went out that day with Rosser," said Timmons. "He must have caught 10 or 12 rainbows in 45 minutes or an hour. I walked off 50 yards, and he yelled and held up his fly rod and showed a double strike. He was one of the best in western North Carolina. I went out that afternoon and caught five or six, which I thought was pretty good for a beginner."

Once in his three decades of trout fishing, the Atlantan had a triple strike.

The Fever Is Contagious

During the early 1950s, relatively few people fished for trout in the north Georgia mountain streams. Many serious anglers thought they had to bait hooks or cast artificial lures in North Carolina and Tennessee rivers to catch a rainbow trout worthy of their den walls. Affluent anglers traveled to the West and Alaska in search of trophies.

In recent years, the Georgia Game and Fish Division has been improving the quality of trout fishing in small streams, rivers, and reservoirs so that Georgians can land rainbows, browns, and brook trout closer to home. To support the trout program, the state began requiring fishermen to purchase trout stamps in 1972, along with their fishing licenses, and 62,301 resident stamps were sold that season.

By 1976, the number had risen to only 67,418, but in 1979, a total of 86,972 Georgians purchased trout stamps, an increase of almost 7,000 over the 1978 figure.

Nearly one million trout grown in Georgia's Burton, Buford, and Summerville hatcheries and in federal hatcheries at Rock Creek and Walhalla, South Carolina, were stocked in Georgia mountain streams and lakes in 1980. During the winter, biologists stock Lake Sidney Lanier with 100,000 rainbows.

Hatchery trout ready for stream stocking are about nine inches long—three fish per pound.

By the end of the trout season in October, between 75 and 90 percent of the little trout stocked in a typical mountain stream will have been caught by fishermen using kernels of corn, nightcrawlers, crickets, salmon eggs, spring lizards, spinning lures, and artificial flies.

Georgia has 3,987 miles of primary and secondary trout streams, including very small tributaries, and the state boasts 882 miles of streams at least ten feet wide. Fisheries teams stock 154 streams, some only once a year, but 20 of them weekly.

One of the finest stretches of trout water extends about 40 miles on the Chattahoochee River from Lake Lanier's Buford Dam to the I-285 west bridge in metropolitan Atlanta.

The Tallulah River is one of the most heavily stocked streams, and it also has an excellent population of native trout. Native trout also are numerous in Cooper's Creek, Wildcat Creek, the upper Chattahoochee at Helen, Dick's Creek, Waters Creek, and Moccasin Creek. The state manages Waters Creek as a trophy trout stream, where the minimum size for a keeper rainbow or brown is 22 inches and for brook trout, 18 inches.

Among other rivers with fair to good trout populations are the Chattooga, Hiawassee, Toccoa, Nottely, Chestatee, Jacks, Conasauga, and Coleman.

Information about trout regulations, streams, and wildlife management areas may be obtained in a brochure available at the Georgia Department of Natural Resources offices in the Trinity-Washington Building near the Capitol in Atlanta.

IV
Crappie

Norman "Korndog" Perry was very surprised to discover that this crappie had struck not only his little jig but also the author's bait while they were trolling in a reservoir.

Mr. and Mrs. Papermouth

After the sun goes down at the end of a scorching day in June or July, the crickets begin chirping in brush and grass on the banks, frogs croak at the water's edge, and lightning bugs by the thousands turn on their taillights in the forest. The sky seems bigger than it ever did back in the city as countless stars twinkle with a faint and friendly glow.

Night has come on a big reservoir in the South, and the folks in boats under bridges have turned on their lanterns and gotten down to serious business. At these bridge parties, nobody has time to deal a hand of cards. The name of the game is to bait a hook with a small minnow and catch another black or white crappie.

During the day on the same lakes, other men and women anchor their boats next to fallen trees, standing timber, and brush piles, but they're not interested in forestry. They, too, are fishing in earnest for crappie.

Bass anglers are more conspicuous in their fast, expensive, gadget-filled boats—they spend a lot more money in the fishing tackle stores. Their tactics and catches appear to gobble up more newspaper space and more television time.

However, the crappie fishermen usually outnumber them by far on a typical spring or summer day, and it's pretty evident which species of fish actually is the most popular.

The crappie is a very prolific pan fish, it's quite easy to catch with minnows and little jig flies, and it certainly is one of the most delicious fish found in southern lakes and rivers.

I suspect the crappie has traveled under more names than anyone on the FBI's Ten Most Wanted list.

In Florida many fishermen call the crappie a speckled perch. I heard it called a sun trout years ago in south Georgia, and in central Georgia some fishermen still speak of the fish as a white perch. The crappie's silver sides and dark blotches or bands have earned another name, calico bass. A fishing buddy from a northern state used to call it the bachelor perch.

The crappie has quite a tender mouth, and if a fisherman sets the hook with too much force, the hook tears out, therefore, the crappie is known in some quarters as the papermouth.

The black crappie has an arched, black or olive back, silver sides with dark-colored blotches, and seven or eight dorsal spines and six anal spines. An easy way to tell the difference between the two is that the white crappie has only six spines on its dorsal fin.

On the silvery sides of the white crappie are spots and dark vertical bands, and its body is more elongated than that of the black crappie.

A Crappie Champion

Carl Sasser of Augusta, Georgia, has fished for crappie many years on 71,533-acre Clarks Hill Lake, backed up by the Savannah River on the Georgia-South Carolina boundary. If you know anybody who has yanked more crappie out of Clarks Hill than Sasser, I'd like to meet them.

Sasser enjoys consistent success in crappie fishing for three principal reasons: he sort of thinks like a crappie, imagining where they would like to be in each season; he fishes at the proper depth; and he knows the locations of four dozen or more big brush piles and areas with submerged standing timber.

Fishing with small minnows, he sometimes enjoys an exciting bonus—hooking largemouth bass on the prowl for lunch around the sunken trees. I was surprised to learn that he apparently held the lake record for largemouth bass. On Valentine's Day in 1972, while crappie fishing, he caught a 14 lb. 14 oz. black bass. I can imagine that must have been a battle royal on his Zebco 33 spin-cast reel, a very limber, seven-foot fiberglass rod, ten-pound test monofilament line, and a No. 2 hook.

Each year Sasser pulls thousands of crappie out of his honey holes in the Little River arm of Clarks Hill, and many of them are in the three- to nearly four-pound class. His personal record for crappie was a four and a half-pound beauty.

In one day, Sasser and three friends caught 602 crappie with

92-dozen minnows, keeping their limits and releasing the others. It's quite an ordinary thing for him and his partner to put 100 crappie in the boat.

"I fish every month of the year," he said. "When the crappie are bedding, I fish right into the banks. In the middle of the summer or winter, I may be fishing in open water. But, except when they are bedding, they stay year-round 16 or 17 feet deep. Even in the winter, they will be the same depth."

He fishes only with live bait—small minnows—and prefers to wet his hooks only between 1 P.M. and dark. If the weather is favorable, he will fish four to six times in a week.

"The moon makes no difference," said Sasser. "In open water I fish with a No. 2 hook, a No. 4 lead eight inches above the hook, and no cork. The only time I use a cork is when I am fishing with my fly rod in shallow water in the spring when they're bedding."

On the day we met, he observed that crappie in Clarks Hill had moved from deep water into shallow areas, and he caught his limit in brush piles six feet deep.

"I hook the minnow straight through the middle of the back at the dorsal fin," he said. "I don't hook the lip or tail. He'll live plenty long the way I hook him. So many use Doll Flies and boo-coos of things. But my minnows always prove best."

Sasser figures he's caught just about every species of fish in the Corps of Engineers reservoir. He sometimes runs into a streak of white bass success, boating fish up to three pounds each. He also has hooked hybrid bass (a cross between a female striped bass and a male white bass), catfish, carp, and even one brown trout.

When Clarks Hill's level drops several feet, the crappie are unable to reach brush piles near the banks in many areas, and Sasser enjoys a distinct advantage over other anglers with his 15- to 20-foot honey holes.

"They've got to go to my places," he said. "They've got no choice."

In the late winter and early spring, the crappie move into

shallow water in a pre-bedding pattern. Sasser locates them on nests from five days before the full moon until four days after.

When Sasser anchors his 18-foot runabout over a brush pile, he learns quickly whether that area will be productive.

"I know how long it takes crappie to bite," he said, laughing. "It only takes two minutes. If I am in one place five minutes without a bite, I know it's time to move the bait or go to another brush pile.

"I might move three or four times in one afternoon. Maybe even five. I figure there are always some hungry crappie in the school. Last year we caught 404 crappie off one brush pile without moving the boat. We used 30-dozen minnows.

"I've seen a feeding period continue half a day. Sometimes I pull into one place and fish until dark, and they never stop biting. Again, though, it may not be over 30 minutes."

His most highly productive fishing period runs between February and October, and he manages to take his limits in the hottest days of the summer when many other fishermen are complaining, "They've got lockjaw."

Smiling Minnows Are Best

One morning in Everett Beal's drug store in Gainesville, Georgia, several fishermen were comparing their scores on nearby Lake Sidney Lanier. One of them shook his head and confessed he barely caught enough crappie to grease his skillet.

Billy Nichols, a truck driver, chuckled and said, "You must have been using ugly minnows. That's what was wrong. When I go to the bait shop, I push the ugly minnows aside. I want the pretty ones.

"I look for pretty minnows with smiles on their faces. They know I'm gonna use them, and I know they'll smile when I get back to the lake and put them on my hooks."

A tall, heavy-set, bewhiskered guy who looks strong enough to wrestle a bear, Nichols fishes for crappie in Lanier every day that he doesn't have a load to haul in his tractor-trailer rig.

He prefers an ultra-light spinning reel, limber fiberglass rod, and six-pound test line. Several inches above a gold No. 4 hook, he pinches a little split shot on his line. He fishes tight-line style without a cork.

"I either fish under a bridge or look for the tree tops," he said. "How deep? I just put my minnow on the bottom and start bringing it up. After I catch the first crappie, I know how many times I need to turn the reel handle next time to get the minnow at the right depth again."

After watching a man in another boat under a bridge pull out his limit of crappie on gold hooks baited with minnows when he had only fair success with dark hooks, Nichols concluded the shiny gold hooks perhaps made a difference.

"I've had people fish with me, and they used a dark hook," he said, "and I'd use the gold hook and catch 25 or 30 fish and they might catch one."

The biggest crappie that Nichols ever caught in Lanier weighed 3 lb. 9 oz.; he feels certain the 38,000-acre lake, fed by the Chattahoochee and Chestatee rivers, is home of some four-pounders.

Nichols figures some folks fail to catch a mess of crappie for two reasons. They don't put their baits at the right depth, and they don't stay on the lake long enough.

"I've gone out on Lanier at twelve noon and at two in the morning, I was still fishing," he said. "My wife sent the Coast Guard lookin' for me. She thought I had drowned. I told my brother-in-law, if you go out there and stay 24 hours, sometime in that 24 hours you'll catch crappie."

Cold weather doesn't seem to affect his style of fishing around boat docks on the north Georgia lake.

"I fish when the water's mighty cold, too, and the crappie still bite," said the truck driver. "I've taken heaters and plugged them onto the dock when it was 18 or 19 degrees."

He used to hook a minnow back of the dorsal fin, but the bait wouldn't survive long. Then a commercial fisherman gave him a good tip.

"Now I run that gold hook through the eye of the minnow, and they'll stay alive longer," he said. "A commercial fisherman told me a fish hits the minnow from the front.

"You put that hook anywhere except the eye or nose, and the fish has to get the whole minnow in his mouth before he's caught. The minute that crappie hits my minnow, I set the hook, and I've got him."

Nichols believes that a crappie fights much better in the winter than in the summer.

"In the winter, I think a crappie is just as strong as a bass," he said. "In that cool water, he'll raise cain like a bream or a bass. In the summer, he'll lay over on his side and you reel him in like he's dead."

Deadly Little Jigs

For many years, anglers have caught crappie on artificial lures, especially the little lead-head jigs with colored hair, in the big impoundments where Mr. and Mrs. Papermouth and their kinfolk are so abundant.

The first small crappie jig that I ever used was the Doll Fly, made by Elmer "Doll" Thompson of Knoxville, Tennessee. Back in those days, I tried a white Doll Fly when the water was very clear, and when it was a bit stained, I figured the yellow Doll Fly would produce some action. It never crossed my mind that a different color pattern ever would be necessary.

My friends and I would work the Doll Flies 1½ to 3 feet under a bobber, casting the lures to the shoreline and next to fallen trees, then bringing them back on a steady but slow retrieve. Sometimes we twitched the rod tip and paused, hoping a crappie would think he had seen a darting minnow. The Doll Flies not only attracted plenty of crappie, but occasionally they drew strikes from largemouth and white bass.

Later, a fishing pal showed me how he cast the Doll Fly without a bobber and retrieved it very slowly next to fallen trees or stumps.

On a windy day in May on Georgia's Lake Jackson, a Macon friend, a man from Monticello, and I stood on a rocky point and cast little, yellow jigs. To allow for longer casts, we pinched a split shot onto the line several inches above the lure.

The lure was retrieved so slowly that it was moving just off the bottom. The wind was strong enough to blow the little bait six or more feet to the side on a cast.

Sometimes the crappie's strike felt like a little tap on the line, and on one cast I felt three thumps before the hook was set, indicating perhaps that more than one fish was hitting it.

My best fish that afternoon was a two-pound crappie, which hit hard and ran to my left, determined not to leave its neighborhood in Lake Jackson. The fiberglass rod bent so sharply that my partners thought a bass had grabbed the lure.

In two hours of casting from that rocky point and shoreline, we caught 80 crappie that weighed a total of 40 pounds. Although the average weight of the fish wasn't bragging material, the fish were real winners when covered with corn meal and fried in deep fat.

Trolling, Casting, and Dipping

A fellow would have to log a lot of miles on his boat or car before meeting anyone who is a more highly skilled crappie angler than Harold L. Barber of Morrow, Georgia, an Atlanta suburb. Fifteen years ago, he was an ardent fly fisherman who made popping bugs in his spare time and enjoyed outwitting largemouth bass and bluegills.

He uses a technique that is far different from the traditional method of catching crappie on a hook baited with a little minnow.

On his favorite lakes—Jackson, Lanier, and Walter F. George in Georgia and Crescent and Toho in Florida—he drifts with the wind in his boat or trolls slowly with an electric motor, pulling a little jig that he designed and named the Hal Fly.

Barber invited me to go fishing on Jackson with him and demonstrated his extremely effective technique. He used a couple of ultra-light spinning reels, fiberglass rods so light in action that a bumble bee could bend them, and six-pound test monofilament line. One rod was in a metal holder on the stern next to his 20 hp outboard motor, while the other was secured within easy reach on the left side of his boat.

"It's best to put the rod in a holder instead of holding it in your hand," Barber said as we drifted across a point. "The normal reaction of a fisherman is to strike when the crappie hits. That's a fatal error.

"When the boat is drifting, slowly moving along, you would be over-reacting and taking the jig away from him. When a crappie strikes this Hal Fly and you jerk the rod a foot or two, he'll drop it. Don't bother the rod until the crappie puts a bow in it. The fish will hook himself."

Looking intently at small, orange blips appearing on the screen of his electronic depth finder, he observed, "We're passing over schools of crappie. One school is at seven feet, another at nine feet."

Within seconds he picked up his sharply-bending spinning rod and pulled in a crappie that had mistaken a passing Hal Fly for a threadfin shad.

The tip of my spinning rod twitched once, and when I grabbed it and tried to set the hook, I missed the strike. Then I remembered his advice and learned a lesson from the experience.

"The wind has changed direction," Barber noted. "You should always remember that when using this technique of fishing for crappie with little jigs, you must go with the wind, not against it. The schools of crappie are facing in the direction the wind is coming from and waiting for food. See the boat over there trolling against the wind? That's a mistake. They won't catch many crappie."

While trolling over some treetops that were several feet beneath the surface, I hooked a crappie that struck harder than I had expected, and the scrappy rascal put a respectable bow in my rod. With an ultra-light spinning rig, a person can more fully appreciate the fighting qualities of this fish. A very stout pole or a medium action rod and heavier reel would deny much of the pleasure and lead a person to suspect the crappie is a weakling.

Barber's 1/16-ounce Hal Fly runs seven or eight feet deep when trolled slowly on six-pound test line with the rod parallel to the water.

"My best day crappie fishing was on January 15, 1971," he said. "My party caught 140 crappie in four and a half hours.

None weighed under ½ pound. It took three men to hold the stringers."

Color is an important factor to consider when fishing with the small jigs, which may be adorned with hair, feathers, or a soft plastic grub tail. The choice of color is dependent upon the season and water conditions.

"In September and early October, I like a little jig that has a black head and white body," said Barber, a native of Arkansas. "I change to a yellow-and-white Hal Fly in November and December. In the last part of December through January, I use a red, green, and yellow Hal Fly. Normally I won't fish much in February after the water temperatures drop below 54 degrees."

The crappie become very inactive, their metabolism drops, and, subsequently, their food requirements are extremely low when the water is cold in the winter.

His experiments on Lake Jackson, 50 miles southeast of Atlanta, showed that crappie stop feeding when the water is 46 degrees at a depth of six feet.

Barber began fishing in the Saline River when he was a youngster in Arkansas—"when I took three steps to my Dad's one." He started making popping bugs for fly fishing in 1951, and designed his first crappie jigs in 1/16- and 1/24-ounce sizes in 1965. Over the next 15 years, he designed a variety of small jigs in numerous color patterns that were good baits, not only for crappie, but also for white bass, largemouth bass, hybrid bass, and striped bass. Bluegills and shellcrackers occasionally take the baits, too.

"In the summer, I find crappie suspended—sometimes 11 to 13 feet deep," said Barber. "I use two white jigs about eight inches apart, cast them out and let them sink before starting the retrieve.

"When you are drifting with the little jigs, the wind won't drift the boat too fast. I use the electric motor to correct the angle of the boat and keep the line straight out.

"Keep the rod tip low. You want the jig to come through the water as steady and consistent as possible with little variation of movement. Give him an opportunity on ultra-light tackle, and you'll find him about as good a fighting fish for his weight as you want. Weight-wise, a crappie won't pull as well as a bream, but in a school a crappie is a vicious, ferocious-hitting fish. He bites with authority and is strictly a game fish as far as I am concerned."

When Barber is fishing for crappie in central and south Florida lakes, he sometimes uses a Hal Fly with a white head, black body, and blue tail or one in the red-green-yellow pattern. He said the best all-round pattern Hal Fly for Florida waters for several years, however, has been the jig with a white head, blue body, and white tail in the 1/12-ounce size. In Georgia, that color pattern is recommended in 1/16 ounce.

On the day we fished, he cautioned me not to pull a knot against the eye of the little jig's hook because it would affect its action. He demonstrated how to tie a Hal Fly loop knot.

"Run the line through the eye of the hook and bring the line up the main line ten inches," he said. "Hold the two strands together. Grasp the jig and form a circle, and drop the jig through the circle.

"Hold the two strands of the circle next to the jig between your index finger and your thumb. Hold tight and pull the knot down as small as you can. Some call it a granny and others a single overhand. Try to make the loop shorter than the distance between the eye of the hook and the point of the hook."

A person could fish the little jigs on a cane pole, but he would have to pinch lead weights onto his monofilament line to make the lure run at the right depth to reach the fish.

Barber said, "In Florida, in lakes where the water is ten feet or less, most fish will be six inches to one foot off the bottom most of the time. Place your weight no closer than 18 inches to the jig. In Crescent Lake, some have adopted the following with cane poles:

"Put on about eight to ten feet of twelve-pound test line. On the last part of this line, put on five large split shots, spaced four inches apart. Tie on 20 or 30 inches of six-pound test line;

Harold Barber enjoys trolling for crappie with Hal Flies, small jigs that he designed, in southern reservoirs.

attach a Hal Fly Dina Mite jig. Never use swivels or other metal objects on the end of this line. Tie the jig directly to the end of the line. Some use a live minnow, lip-hooked on the jig. In the Kissimmee chain of lakes, they use one large shot and eight-pound test line."

* * *

Wesley Leverett, a lieutenant in the DeKalb County, Georgia, police department, enjoys fishing for crappie with the little jig flies. In January and early February, he fishes with the red, green, and yellow Hal Fly weighing 1/24 ounce, then in mid-February switches to a yellow-and-white jig.

"I try to fish mostly in water where you have visibility of 18 inches to two feet, but I have caught them in water a little muddy," he said. "You'll usually catch crappie from eight to twelve feet deep in stump coves."

If he gets more than one strike while trolling the jigs, he circles in his boat and passes over the area again.

He said, "Usually I just pick me a bank and run the whole bank trying to find crappie. You can catch them this year where you found them last year. They'll hit more viciously in March and later in the spring. I feel that a fisherman definitely can catch more crappie trolling with these little lures than staying in one spot and fishing with minnows."

* * *

One miserably cold winter day when I had the blues and longed for my favorite season, spring, I called Harold Barber and asked him how on earth he would catch a crappie in that frigid water in Jackson or Lanier.

He reminded me it was the season to go dipping.

In deep, clear Lake Lanier in the winter, the crappie will be lying at depths of 35 feet or more, while in a shallower lake such as Jackson, they may inhabit 20-foot levels. Submerged brush and trees at 9 to 11 feet next to boat docks may attract crappie in Georgia's Lake Jackson or Sinclair. I have hooked crappie while jigging silver spoons for bass at 45 to 55 feet.

For the jig-dipping method, Barber prefers an ultra-light spinning reel and rod, six-pound test line and Hal Flies weighing 1/16 and 1/24 ounce.

"In dipping, the smallest lure you can come up with will catch more crappie. They don't want it. They are more curious than hungry. They just bump it. The best colors are the greens and blues. I like a white or yellow combination with green or blue. My favorite is the fluorescent or radiant green with a white or red head, a blue or green middle and a white or a yellow tail."

In the relatively clear lower end of Lanier, the productive patterns are yellow head, yellow body, and white tail, the white-green-white, and the white-blue-white.

Cast the little jig the same number of feet that you think the crappie are lying under the boat, and allow it to sink until the line is in a vertical position near bridge pilings, in brush, and in tree tops, Barber recommended. The jig also could be lowered by pulling line off the reel's spool.

Barber doesn't twitch or raise the rod tip to give the Hal Flies action of a crippled or dying shad. Instead, he gathers in the line with his left hand and moves the jig up and down.

"I try to let it off and put the Hal Fly below where the school of crappie is. Get the lure below the school and bring it up through it. A crappie will never go down after the lure or minnow. He will come up after it."

When Barber is dipping for crappie, he favors a jig that has a feather or chicken hackle tail rather than marabou.

"If the feather-tail jig is tied properly, two feathers oppose each other," he said, "and they move to each other. The feathers then relax and move away from each other in an undulating action.

"The crappie don't want it to move fast. You move the jig a little, and the feathers close together. The feathers open up and come apart the same as a breathing fish does. The crappie don't like erratic movement of the bait. They like it smooth and easy. You never touch the reel handle dipping the Hal Fly. Use your left hand. The crappie hit it on the rise and fall."

If the jig is moved horizontally in a brush pile or tree top, odds are good that it will become hung on a limb.

Crappie hooked in the winter will "run pretty good size," many of them weighing between one and two pounds and carrying eggs in their early stage of development.

"I start dipping my Hal Flies when the water temperature drops below 58 degrees," said Barber. "Above 58 degrees, I could troll them behind an electric motor. In the dead of winter, the strike is just a little tap. Watch the line go slack or feel a little tick on the line. In winter they probably don't eat 25 percent of the amount of food they need in spring and summer."

The Georgian has found that crappie are most active in water temperatures ranging from 62 to 76 degrees.

Trophy Almost Became a Meal

Bobby G. Etheridge of Jonesboro took a long look at the old rod and spinning reel that his brother-in-law, Steve Cheek, of East Point, Georgia, brought to Lake Spivey for an afternoon of fishing in March, 1975. "Man, you don't have much to fish with," Ethridge said.

The rod and reel, which Cheek had found on a lake bank about five years earlier, were in bad condition and still had the original monofilament line with a couple of knots in it. While Etheridge did some work in his yard, Cheek and his little sister fished from the dock, baiting their little hooks with minnows in hopes the crappie would bite.

"My cork went under pretty good," said Cheek. "The fish ran a good bit and then got tangled up in a little tree in front of the dock. I asked my sister to hold the rod and reel, and I got in the boat and got the fish out with the landing net."

The fish that Cheek pulled out of the Georgia lake was a 4 lb. 4 oz. black crappie, equal in weight to the state record taken by Shirley Lavender near Athens in June, 1971. His fish was 19 inches long and had a girth of 16⅝ inches.

The world record black crappie tipped the scales at six pounds and was caught November 28, 1969, in Sea Plane Canal at Westwego, Louisiana, by Lettie Theresa Robertson. In July, 1957, the world record white crappie, weighing 5 lb. 3 oz., was landed in Enid Lake in Mississippi.

"When I caught the fish, I thought I'd got a nice supper here," said Cheek.

Etheridge said, "He was going to take him home and eat him. I told him, 'You might fish for 20 years without seeing a crappie that big.' "

Cheek decided to have his big crappie mounted by a taxidermist, and he entered the catch in a Georgia fishing contest.

"I just got lucky," said Cheek. "I haven't been fishing a whole lot. I have fished three days this year, and I'm just getting started fishing lately. I was lucky as the dickens. The rod and reel were real old and in bad shape."

A heating and air conditioning mechanic at a hospital, he said his largest crappie previously was a fish weighing a little over one pound.

Etheridge told me that he baited his hook with red wigglers to catch a 4 lb. 2 oz. crappie in Georgia's Lake Nottely about 25 years ago.

V

Redbreast

Royalty of River Pan Fish

If the bluegill reigns as the king and queen of the pan fish in farm ponds and other small lakes, then the redbreast sunfish certainly are the royalty of the rivers.

I have respected these brightly-colored, scrappy fish highly since my high school years in Waycross, Georgia, when my father and our friends caught them during the spring and summer in Georgia and Florida rivers.

Fancy, high-priced fishing tackle isn't required to catch a big mess of redbreast when they are spawning. You only need line, hooks, sinkers, lively worms, and bushes on the banks.

When Ed Lary, Jr., and I were walking home from high school in Waycross on a hot afternoon in May, 1949, he said, "Harold's daddy says the redbellies are going on the beds in the Satilla River."

Homework obviously ranked considerably lower than the redbellies in our priorities, so we hopped into the Lary family's old maroon Plymouth, bought two cups of earthworms, and headed out a sandy road several miles to the Satilla, one of the most crooked and lovely streams that the good Lord ever created.

After parking the car in the woods, we walked down a path to the sandy bank of the river, then stepped very quietly to the next bend, looking at the shallow water and searching for saucer-shaped nests made by the romantic redbreasts.

Each time that we discovered a bed, we cut a three- or four-foot piece of braided line, tied one end to a bush, squeezed on a BB-sized sinker with pliers, baited a No. 8 hook with a worm and dropped the hook into the middle of the nest. There usually wasn't sufficient time to set out two or three more bush lines before we would hear a splash, turn around and see a small limb thrashing on the surface like a whip as a redbelly tugged with all its might trying to gain his freedom.

Reminiscing years later about those happy days of river fishing, Ed said, "Our friend Harold Tanner's father, Carey Tanner, had taught me to catch redbreast this way. When the redbreast were bedding, it wasn't hard to find beds close to the bank. That day you and I fished three or four bends of the Satilla and caught 35 or 40 redbreast that weighed between ½ pound and 1 pound each."

Sometimes when we walked around a bend to rig more bush lines, the redbreast would return to their nests and steal the bait, but our batting average was pretty good, and we occasionally saw two bushes waving with hooked fish at the same time.

If a male redbreast was guarding the nest when we walked up, the fish would be frightened away as we baited a hook, but moments after we walked down the bank, he would slip cautiously back to the bed and pick up the worm. A female redbreast depositing eggs in the cleared spot next to the bank would be spooked by our presence but would also return soon and grab the bait.

Ed used to attribute part of his fishing success to the fact that he chewed loose-leaf tobacco, explaining, "A little tobacco juice on the bait always makes 'em bite better. You ought to try it, Charles, and see how it works."

I'll try a lot of things to catch fish, but chewing tobacco is last on my list of piscatorial tricks.

My father sometimes fished for redbreast from a sandbar in the Satilla. He would bait a No. 6 or No. 8 hook with a worm, pinch on his line a couple of BB leads and add an egg-shaped sliding sinker for enough additional weight to enable him to cast far out into the river. After the bait settled on the sandy bottom, he propped his fishing rod in the fork of a limb that he had stuck in the ground. If a person set out two such rigs and got bites on both, he might wonder which way to turn.

Don't pinch onto your line a heavy piece of lead, because the redbreast might be wary after pulling against that weight and drop the bait. The line passes easily through the hole in a slip sinker lying on the bottom, and the fish doesn't become suspicious.

Dad and I fished for redbreast many Saturdays in a 14-foot, flat-bottom, plywood johnboat in creeks that flow into the gorgeous St. Marys River, which forms a sort of heel-shaped boundary between Georgia and Florida after the water meanders out of the Okefenokee Swamp.

We baited our small hooks with red wigglers and, in late summer, with juicy and quite messy catalpa worms. Some folks in south Georgia insist that a catalpa worm must be turned inside out to get best results in fishing for redbreast and bluegills, but I never bought that idea. Who's got time to stop and wash his hands 50 times when the fish are biting?

Later, Dad became an enthusiastic and very skilled fly fisherman, and he caught a tremendous number of redbreast and bluegills on little popping bugs. If the rascals wouldn't strike the yellow or the chartreuse poppers, you might just as well go home. Yearling largemouth bass also would pounce on the little popping bugs, and it took some skill and luck to keep them from cutting the monofilament leader on a snag or fallen tree in a creek.

One afternoon on the St. Marys we saw the mouth of a very big bowfin open under a yellow popper on the surface, and a fraction of a second later Dad jerked his little lure away.

Dad remarked, "I wasn't worried so much about losing one popping bug, but that big mudfish [bowfin] might have done some damage to my bamboo fly rod."

Although cane poles are still widely used in fishing for redbreast, the majority of fishermen today prefer either a closed-face spinner (a push-button reel) or an open-face spinning reel with six- to ten-pound test monofilament line. Catching a hand-size redbreast can be great fun if you mount one of these reels on a light or ultra-light action five- to seven-foot fiberglass or graphite rod. And, these reels make it possible to cover a much greater amount of water.

Set the drag so that a small amount of pressure from a fish can make the line slip off the spool, and you can enjoy every ounce of the pan fish as it turns its broad side to you and tugs and battles for its life.

Some anglers do not enjoy the pan fish's fight to the fullest because they are using line of excessive test-strength and fishing rods that are much too stiff in action. I like to see a redbreast bend an ultra-light action rod into a very sharp bow; it's a mighty good feeling, too.

Beginning fishermen sometimes make the mistake of using too large a hook for redbellies. A No. 8 hook is the most popular size, and it certainly will handle a great, great grandmama redbreast, but some awfully little fish will be caught on it. You can discourage those "butterbean-size" fish by using a No. 6 hook.

Bug pole fishing for pan fish continues to grow more popular each spring on the rivers. It's a form of angling similar to fly fishing and even deadlier sometimes.

One of my fishing friends in Waycross, Georgia, Revenal Winge, says that bug pole fishing first became "an open secret" among fishermen about 25 years ago in southeast Georgia.

Sizes of the rigs will vary slightly, but a typical one would be an 11-foot bamboo pole with 14 feet of at least 12-pound test monofilament line. The pan fish pros generally agree that it's best to use a line that is three feet longer than the pole.

The artificial lures are little popping bugs in a variety of colors with No. 6 or No. 8 hooks; the No. 6 hook is desirable if a largemouth bass takes a swat at the bug.

Select a bamboo pole that has slightly more backbone than a

fly rod but is limber enough to whip the bug toward the bank in fly-fishing style.

When you're fly fishing in a farm pond, you usually cast a fairly good distance in order to keep from spooking the fish. In bug pole fishing as you drift down a river, you can work the bait when the boat is closer to the bank and drop the bug into rather tight spots next to snags, bushes, stumps, and blown-down trees.

On such a float trip, you'll probably make more casts and hit even more of the likely spots than a fly fisherman, and, with some practice, you could become more accurate than a friend casting with the long rod.

Using 12-pound test line makes it possible for a person to pull fully-grown, fat redbreast out of rough, snaggy areas without much trouble. But, if Uncle Ned or Old Nelly, a humongous largemouth bass, takes a notion to inhale the popping bug, you might hook more than you can handle.

The little popping bugs not only attract strikes from redbreast, bluegills, and bass, but also from crappie, other sunfish, chain pickerel, and an occasional bowfin.

Fishermen using the bug poles with accuracy have brought home big strings of redbreast and bream from the Satilla, St. Marys, Flint, Suwannee, Altamaha, Ogeechee, and Alapaha Rivers. Pan fish also have been taken on the bug poles in Georgia's Okefenokee Swamp.

In the spring, cast the bug close to stumps, logs, and brush at the edge of the river bank, and let it lie motionless a few seconds, giving the fish time to make up its mind whether to hit. Then twitch the bug gently to make a slight ripple on the surface.

When the water is much warmer in the summer, the redbreast and bluegills often prefer to see the bug "travel" a little across the surface.

To produce such action, shake your wrist and raise the tip of the pole a bit, causing the bug to appear to walk across the water. This requires practice and patience to make the little bait imitate natural movement of an insect. You must convince the fish this bug is the real thing, not a little piece of cork that a guy with fishing fever tossed into the water.

R. Vaughn Snow, a retired Waycross businessman, has enjoyed for many years an angling technique that he calls "pitch fishing."

"In pitch fishing," he said, "I like to use a nine-foot fly rod with a four-foot leader and a very small split shot, a No. 8 hook and a cricket. I cast it close to the banks, but sometimes I have to roll it under the bushes and overhanging tree limbs.

"You roll the line deep in there to reach the fish. If there are lots of close places, thick bushes, I use a 7½-foot or 8-foot fly rod."

He pitch fishes for bluegills in the small farm ponds and for redbreast in the southeast Georgia rivers.

"One afternoon in the spring, my partner and I caught 70 bluegills in a pond," he said. "Another day I caught 20 bream that weighed a total of 22 pounds. I weighed what looked like the five biggest bream, and they averaged 1½ pounds."

Snow offered some good advice on how to pitch fish with a fly rod.

"Stay out of the bushes and trees," he said chuckling. "You can't catch 'em in a tree. But, you do need to cast as close to the banks as possible to put your bait near the fish.

"Most people probably fish a little too fast. If I'm using a popping bug on a fly rod, I cast it out and let it lie there. Then I shake it a little and make it wiggle. Sometimes a bream will lie there and look at it before it decides to strike."

The redbreast, found in rivers throughout the South, has long, black gill flaps, olive to brownish-gray back, blue-and-golden side, and a yellow, bright-orange, or red belly. Between the mouth and eye are irregular bluish stripes. A female has brighter colors than a male.

A big catch during the spawning period may include fish ranging from ¼ to ¾ of a pound, and if a person is fortunate enough to boat a one-pounder, he should rush it to a taxidermist's shop.

When water temperatures rise to 68 or 70 degrees in the spring, male redbreast fan saucer-shaped nests three to five inches deep and two to three feet in diameter near trees, stumps, or brush.

After the female deposits 500 to 7,500 eggs, the male releases sperm for fertilization and stays to guard the eggs against predators. The papa moves his fins constantly to keep water circulating over the eggs during the incubation period to prevent them from being suffocated by siltation.

Several years ago, Florida biologists examined food items from stomachs of 979 Suwannee River redbreast and 774 Santa Fe River redbreast. The Suwannee redbreast fed on midge larvae, isopods, caddis fly larvae, little crustaceans, sand fly larvae, beetles, ants, young blue crabs, snails, clams, and small fish.

In the Santa Fe, the redbreast fed on caddis fly and midge larvae, mayfly nymphs, and emergent insects.

A one year creel census on the Suwannee indicated that 38 percent of the fish caught were redbreast, while on the Santa Fe, 53 percent of the hooked fish were redbellies.

The most popular baits used by fishermen were red worms, catalpa worms, oak worms, bonnet worms, and crickets.

VI
Striped Bass

Larry Swicegood holds a big striped bass that he caught after baiting his hook with a bream. His son, Kevin, 9, who also has boated some big stripers, waits patiently for a bite.

Streamlined Champs

By mid-morning the sunshine had taken most of the chill out of the air. It was late October, 1973, when a friend, Tolly Brinkley of Stockbridge, Georgia, and I were casting to the banks for largemouth bass in a cove on Georgia's Lake Sinclair. Leaves were turning yellow, gold, bronze, red, and purple, and I imagined how the mountain roads must be clogged with heavy traffic as leaf-watchers flocked to the autumn show.

I was casting with an ultra-light fiberglass spinning rod, which had willow branch action and had been made by Tolly. Six-pound test monofilament line filled a little spinning reel's spool, and I had tied on a Mepps Spinner with a No. 2 silver blade and squirrel tail, hoping a frisky largemouth would take a notion to eat lunch early.

The spinning lure dropped right on target next to a stump, and I began a slow retrieve, turning the handle half a dozen times before a powerful fish struck so hard that it nearly yanked the rod and reel out of my hands. Fortunately, the drag setting was light, and the fish very easily began stripping yards of line off the spool as she headed for deeper water. The drag was screaming, the rod was bending in a sharp bow, and I was hoping the fish wouldn't make a hard left or right around a snag.

The electric motor on my bass boat's bow slowly moved us away from shore, and I held the rod high, wondering how far that rascal would run and how much punishment that light line could stand. For a while it appeared that the strong fish would steal every yard of my line and reach the Oconee River arm of Sinclair. Finally, she turned, and in the next few minutes I managed to regain a few yards of line, only to see her streak away on another drag-screaming run. The drag setting required a pulling force of two or three pounds for the fish to take line from the spool. I was relieved several minutes later to see signs that the fish was tiring at last. Keeping the line tight, I slowly pumped the rod up and down and pulled the fish nearer the boat. When the fish ran under the boat, I stuck everything but the rod's handle in the water and feared she was a goner.

In a moment I was able to bring the fish to the surface, and Tolly was ready with the landing net. I nervously lit a cigarette, and we admired a handsome striped bass that measured 26 inches in length. Neither of us had any scales, but we estimated the striper's weight at ten pounds.

"If I had hooked that fish's mama or grandmama, we might have been fighting her in this cove until sundown," I told Tolly. "That rascal is much stronger pound for pound than a largemouth." Then, reminiscing about my youth in South Georgia, I recalled stories about striped bass on the St. Marys River that broke lines, snapped fishing rods, and stripped gears of the reels of anglers who were casting or trolling plugs for black bass.

In South Carolina's Santee-Cooper lakes—Lake Marion and Lake Moultrie—anglers caught striped bass that had become landlocked when the dam was constructed in the 1940s. During the 1950s, fisheries biologists collected male and female striped bass from the rivers and began a highly successful hatchery program to produce millions of the offspring for stocking in the Santee-Cooper system.

Today the striped bass is regarded as one of our most prized game fish, and stripers are being caught on live bait and artificial lures in U.S. Army Corps of Engineers and power company reservoirs across the South.

One of the most enthusiastic striper anglers was Tiny Lund, a big, friendly guy from Cross, South Carolina, who enjoyed considerable success on the auto racing circuit. It is a shame that Lund didn't live to see his name in the books as the holder of the world record for landlocked striped bass. Lund was killed in an auto racing accident several years after landing a 55-pound striped bass in Santee-Cooper's Lake Moultrie on January 29, 1963. At that time there wasn't a category for landlocked stripers in the world record listings.

In the spring of 1977, the National Fresh Water Fishing Hall of Fame in Hayward, Wisconsin, notified the South Carolina Wildlife and Marine Resources Department that Lund's catch had been recognized as a world record. The previous record had been a 50-pounder from the Colorado River.

Lund's 55-pound striper was 46½ inches long with a girth of 30⅝ inches and was determined to be 18 years old.

The present I.G.F.A. freshwater, all-tackle, world record striped bass weighing 59 lb. 12 oz. was pulled out of the Colorado River in Arizona in the spring of '77 by Frank W. Smith. Incidentally, Georgia's record striper was even bigger. A 63-pounder was caught in the Oconee River during its spawning run from the Atlantic on May 30, 1967.

Efforts to give Lund's catch the recognition it deserved were intensified in 1976, after a magazine article quoted Lake Havasu marina officials as saying a 50-pounder from the Colorado River was the biggest striper ever landed in the nation.

Jerry Dyer of Santee-Cooper country and state wildlife officials contacted the National Marine Fisheries Service in Washington. Dr. Bob Stevens, with the Fisheries Service, who had certified Lund's catch in 1963, when he was a South Carolina fisheries biologist, signed an affidavit. Two conservation officers who had seen the fish also verified its weight, and an old photograph was found.

Dyer believes anglers might catch even heavier stripers in the Santee-Cooper lakes. In the mid-1960s, a striped bass weighing over 80 pounds washed up on Bonneau Beach, and an 85-pound striper was found dead in Lake Marion near the U.S. 301 and I-95 bridges in the early 1970s.

A Florida fishing friend told me that around the turn of the century, commercial fishermen using hand lines and nets in the Gulf of Mexico brought in striped bass weighing close to a hundred pounds.

Georgia's state record striped bass traveled a long distance from the Atlantic on its spawning run. The 63-pound beauty was caught in the Oconee River near Dublin by Kelley A. Ward in May, 1967. If the fish had continued up the Oconee, it eventually would have found its path blocked by the Lake Sinclair dam near Milledgeville.

"A Whole New Ball Game"

Jack Wingate, operator of a fishing camp on 37,500-acre Lake Seminole, backed up by the Jim Woodruff dam just over the Georgia line in Florida, summed up the striped bass's "arrival" quite well when he observed, "It's a whole new ball game." He assured me that the striper is a great game fish that a fellow with a heart condition would be wise to avoid hooking.

"This is the kind of fish that can jerk the rod and reel right out of your hands," said Jack, chuckling. "Every now and then we hook somebody's fishing rod and reel on the bottom with a plug and pull it out."

A few days earlier, he said, a Florida angler worked a jointed blue-and-silver Rebel on the surface like a crippled baitfish and hooked a 22 lb. 8 oz. striper.

"They're finding these rockfish—stripers—in deep water near the dam and also schooling and feeding on threadfin shad up the lake. It seems like the schooling stripers run from three to five pounds, and the big ones are roaming around feeding by themselves," he said. "At two o'clock one afternoon, some fishermen found a school of stripers nearly a quarter of a mile long on top of the water tearing up the shad."

Jerry Sims, a fishing guide at Jack's camp, told me that a 38½-pounder was caught on a saltwater size Rebel lure close to the dam.

"Seminole should have a striped bass pushing 50 pounds by

now," said Jerry, who boated a 25½-pounder that hit a Little George. "In 1978, I fought a striper for almost an hour, and I believe he was in the 40-pound range. I was using 20-pound line and a saltwater-size Rapala, and the long, steady, tremendous pressure straightened out those strong treble hooks."

Jerry has been a mighty faithful fan of the black bass, pulling out his limits dozens of days, but he confessed that both the striped bass and hybrid bass (white bass-striper cross) are superior fighters.

"I love the black bass to pieces, but no black bass in the world has the pulling ability of the hybrid and striper," he said. "You could tie one end of line in the jaw of a five-pound largemouth and the other end in the mouth of a five-pound hybrid, and that hybrid would drown the largemouth. If you don't loosen your reel's drag, a big striper will break 20-pound line on the first run. They would almost break well rope on the first run."

If an angler loosens his reel's drag so the line would slip on the fish's run, however, he could catch stripers and hybrids of respectable size on 10- or 12-pound line, but it would take a while to bring him in.

"But that's what it's all about," said Jerry, "having the enjoyment of the fight and realizing how much power that fish you are playing has. We have a lake too shallow for stripers to get in big schools as much as they do in Santee-Cooper lakes. The big stripers are loners until they congregate in front of the dam in October and November.

"Stripers are such voracious feeders. You'll find them by the dozens on your depth finder, and they might not hit any lures in your tackle box. But, ten minutes later, they are up on the surface chasing shad, and all of a sudden there's an acre of fish erupting. In Seminole the best live bait for stripers is a large shad or a live eel."

In the autumn, when stripers congregate near the dam, fishermen also bait their hooks with skipjack, a member of the herring family. Anglers catch them on little white jigs that they cast while standing on the rip-rap. Then they pick up a big spinning reel or baitcasting reel, run a strong hook through the skipjack's lip, and cast it into the water that is slowly moving toward the dam's gates.

Many stripers in the 5- to 20-pound class have been taken by anglers using these skipjack as bait or casting long, cigar-shaped, black-and-silver plugs that resemble this forage fish.

A striped-bass fisherman can get a crick in his neck after watching the birds all morning.

"The birds will tell you something is going on," said Jack Wingate. "They've got nothing to say if they're just sitting on the water. But, if you see them flying and all of a sudden diving into the water, that means the black bass, stripers, hybrids, or white bass are feeding on a school of shad. The gulls rush down to pick up the pieces and leftovers."

"Hey, Where Are We Going?"

Norton H. Murphy, who owns a farm near Bainbridge, Georgia, enjoys fishing in the Flint River arm of Lake Seminole, a gorgeous stretch of that stream ten miles or more north of the impoundment. Over a period of several days of fishing during a recent summer, Murphy lost a number of extremely powerful stripers that ripped free after breaking his monofilament line or straightening treble hooks on his lures.

Figuring he'd better go loaded for bear, he put three larger sets of treble hooks on his Bang-O-Lure, a balsa, cigar-shaped lure in a silver pattern with black stripes, and then checked his 20-pound test line for any kinks or signs of abrasion. Murphy launched his 14-foot aluminum boat in the Flint River on a sizzling July 31, 1980, in the midst of a drought. Casting close to the bank with an Ambassadeur 5000 baitcasting reel, Murphy was not working the lure to imitate a crippled baitfish, but was bringing back the balsa plug with a medium speed retrieve.

"Soon as it hits the water, I start retrieving," he said. "I don't ever stop it. The rest of the stripers hit and stayed underwater. That big striped bass came out of the water and lacked just a few inches of clearing it.

"It was like a tarpon in the Gulf. I was amazed. I just couldn't believe it. It was so big, its mouth was wide open and its gills flared."

Murphy must have had awfully big goose bumps covering his

arms as he watched the 40-pound striped bass crash back to the surface, making a splash like a boulder plummeting into the river.

The great, great, grandmama striper, 43½ inches long with a 27-inch girth, sounded and then dashed into the Flint River channel, picking up speed as it headed downstream.

"I turned on my trolling motor and got my boat out in the middle of the river, all the time fighting him," said Murphy. "The fish was taking line, and I was trying to figure out how in the world to land him. I thought, 'Ain't no way to get him in.'"

As the rugged fish pulled the lightweight aluminum boat, the angler must have felt like yelling, "Hey, where are we going?" Maybe the striper had a ticket for Lake Seminole.

"I looked at my small landing net, and it was hopeless," said Murphy. "I told myself if I got him in shallow water and he decided to do something and I was on the bank, he would just mess me up, and I'd wind up tangled with those hooks."

He feared the strong fish would eventually jerk the rod and reel out of his hands as the river current and the steady pull of the striper slowly carried the boat nearer the next bend in the river. After a battle lasting 45 minutes, the huge fish appeared to be exhausted.

"He finally gave up," said Murphy. "The boat was crossways of the river. The fish was on the north side of the boat, upstream, and the wind was from the south blowing straight up the river.

"I was hanging onto my fishing rod with my left hand and just put my right hand over on him and worked my hand under his gills. He didn't want to open them. I got my fingers in the gills and lifted him into the boat."

The front treble hook on the plug had been straightened, the middle hook was bent, and two barbs of the rear treble hook were embedded in the side of the fish's mouth.

Until that memorable summer day, Murphy's biggest freshwater catches had been an eight-pound largemouth bass and a ten-pound striper. He assured me that the Flint River was the home of even heavier striped bass.

"I hooked one that I believe would put that 40-pounder in the shade," he said. "It hit a Bang-O-Lure. The reel's drag was singing. Finally, can't understand why, that 20-pound line snapped. It sounded like a cap pistol. The line broke right at the reel."

Russ Ober of Albany, Georgia, a state fisheries biologist, wondered whether the 40-pound striper had traveled up the Flint from the Gulf of Mexico several years earlier, was stocked in Seminole as a fingerling, or had hatched in the river.

Lake Seminole is Georgia's only reservoir where reproduction of striped bass has been confirmed. Stripers on spring spawning runs swim up the Flint to a dam at Albany, and the eggs tumbling in the current have sufficient hours to mature and hatch before reaching the flat water of the impoundment.

Two striped bass weighing nearly 50 pounds each were believed to have been netted illegally in the Flint River. Fishing camp operator Jack Wingate said the biggest striper taken on hook and line in Seminole weighed about 38 pounds.

Stripers Love Bluegills

Fisheries biologists say that hungry striped bass are crazy about threadfin shad in the southern reservoirs. The big brutes also have been known to gobble up gizzard shad, eels, young pan fish, rainbow trout, herring, and also largemouth bass, and spotted bass. An Atlanta fisherman told me about fighting for 20 minutes, but finally losing a giant striper that grabbed a 13-inch spotted bass he had hooked on a plastic worm in Lake Sidney Lanier. The striper wasn't hooked; she simply wouldn't let go of the tasty spot. The angler estimated the fish was "at least three feet long when I saw him right at the side of the boat. That's when he spit out the spot and backed off."

Many anglers have learned that the bluegill is a very fine bait for trophy-size striped bass in the reservoirs and rivers.

In 1980, in Elberton, Georgia, I met a nine-year-old boy named Kevin Swicegood, who weighed 70 pounds. In one morning he had caught striped bass that were almost half his own size. The first striper weighed 27 pounds, and the second one was a 29-pound beauty. The strikes came in a 45-minute period on the Savannah River in the upper reaches of Clarks Hill Lake.

The youngster was hoping to break the 30-pound barrier with stripers before his tenth birthday. Don't bet against its happening before the boy gets his driver's license, because the Savannah River is the mailing address of some gigantic, tackle-bustin' stripers.

Kevin didn't have what you'd call beginner's luck. He was exposed to the joys and thrills of angling at a very young, tender age. He accompanied his parents, Mr. and Mrs. Larry Swicegood, to Clarks Hill fishing holes many times before he was old enough to read and write.

On an August morning, he boated an 11 lb. 5 oz. hybrid bass—the white bass-striped bass cross, and he has caught many stripers and largemouth bass.

Kevin's father always fishes with fresh bait, catching about four-finger wide, sometimes a bit bigger, bluegills on worms in shallow water close to the river bank, and keeping them in his bass boat's live well.

A ½-ounce sinker slides along the line above a two-way swivel tied a foot or more from a bass-size hook, which can be stuck through the bream's lip or through the body at the dorsal fin.

After seeing the structure on his depth finder's screen, he lowers the bream into the water next to the boat and watches a tight line instead of a bobber. The bream swims a short distance just off the bottom, and a quivering or twitching rod tip may signal he's getting mighty nervous and scared upon seeing an approaching striped bass or hybrid.

"On the day Kevin caught the two, big stripers, we were fishing on an underwater hill on the edge of the Savannah River channel," said Swicegood. "It's in a bend of the river and is 22 feet deep. The 27-pounder picked up Kevin's bait and started off. Kevin said, 'I've got him, Daddy.' I said, 'Make sure you have the hook set.'"

The fish tried for a moment to stay on the river bottom, then made a strong run into the channel, turned and circled the boat. Kevin held the stiff Browning boron rod's tip high and kept the 20-pound line on the Ambassadeur 4500C reel tight as the striper tugged and fought for its life.

Within several minutes, Kevin was able to pull the fish to the side of the boat, where his father picked it up with a big landing net. Swicegood baited his son's hook with another bream, and a few minutes later the boy was battling another big fish.

"The second fish, the 29-pounder, really showed off," said Swicegood. "That striped bass made long, sustained runs up and down the river channel. I have a 16-foot boat, and that fish was pulling our boat up and down the lake."

"I wasn't afraid Kevin would have the rod jerked out of his hands. He's had a lot of experience and handled some big fish over the years. I knew Kevin wouldn't turn it loose until he was wet—pulled into the river. Each of those fish was 42 inches long."

The boy told me he believed that a striped bass, pound for pound, pulls much harder than a largemouth bass.

"You just can't pick it up," he said of a bulldogging or running striper. "The big fish struck, and the bream just bumped, and he took off. He ran around the boat and stayed down. I saw him later about three feet down in the water. I said, 'Oh, no. He's so big.'"

The same day Kevin enjoyed fighting those fish, one of their friends, Jack McConnell, pulled out a 31-pound striper within sight of their boat.

Swicegood said the secret of Kevin's success "is just going fishing often and being very observant."

Kevin feels that it would be very satisfying to earn a living by catching fish.

"Maybe I'll be a professional fisherman," he said. "I would like to fish every day of the week."

New Reel Passes Test

Jeff DeVore, 14, of Decatur, Georgia, walked to the end of a diving board on the boat dock at Lake Lanier after tying on a small, broken-back Rebel. He couldn't wait to try out a new closed-face reel and rod that his parents had given him that spring morning. On his second cast into open water in the cove, he turned the Zebco 33 reel's handle half a dozen times and suddenly felt a shoulder-jarring strike.

"He almost pulled me in," said Jeff. "After he tugged the first time, I got off the diving board. I was afraid he would pull me in."

This was a wise move, because the teenager had hooked a 27-pound, 37-inch-long striped bass, a record size at that time for Lanier. On its first run, the striped bass took nearly all of the ten-pound line.

"I didn't know how much line I had," said Jeff. "He just kept running. I was waiting for it to run out of line. Finally the fish stopped. I'd reel him in about ten yards, and then he'd take off again. He did that three times."

Almost 15 minutes later, as his parents watched and waited in suspense, wondering what on earth was on the end of the line, the boy managed to work the fish to within a few feet of the dock, and the striper rolled and boiled on the surface.

"It looked like a monster," the boy said. "I ain't never seen nothing like it. I ran off the dock and to the bank."

His father waded into the shallow, cold water that March day, and carefully picked up the trophy. A small treble hook on the black-and-silver Rebel was lodged securely in the fish's lower jaw; the hook wasn't even bent, perhaps because of a light setting on the reel's drag.

Mrs. DeVore said, "We were so excited. I didn't know the fish was that big. I tell you, I didn't react much until I saw the fish in the water. I thought Jeff had caught something that didn't belong in the lake. It looked like something from the sea. My husband explained it was a saltwater fish."

Jeff said, "Before this, my biggest fish was about a three-pound catfish. My biggest bass was about a pound. I'm going to put this fish on the wall."

Schooling Stripers—
A Thrill a Minute

Howard Moncus of Atlanta and his wife, Mary, were fishing with plastic worms for largemouth bass on a point in the Alcovy River section of Georgia's Lake Jackson. At eight o'clock that morning, he saw a striped bass break the surface in attacking a school of threadfin shad.

He quickly picked up another rod and reel and cast a Hot Spot, a crank bait that imitates a shad, into the area where the fish was feeding.

"He stopped it, I tell you," said Moncus. "It must have taken me five minutes to get him in. He stripped off a lot of that 14-pound line, and I didn't think for a while I'd get him."

The striped bass weighed 15 lb. 6 oz., and was the first of 15 stripers, the smallest weighing six pounds, that were hooked and boated in an hour of action-packed fishing.

They released three fish and returned to Walker Harris Marina with 12 stripers that weighed a total of 119 pounds on Willie Allen's groaning scales.

Moncus, admitting that his wrists and arms were worn to a frazzle, said, "All of them were caught on Hot Spots. The line broke twice, and two got taken away from me. I would crank the plug, hesitate and let it fall, and then crank again. I was casting to the edge of a ledge, and the water there was about 30 feet deep. The striped bass just stayed there feeding on the shad."

The color of the lures didn't seem to matter while the stripers were in a feeding frenzy. Moncus caught the first and biggest striper on a Hot Spot with a bone-and-orange finish, and the other plugs were gray with black backs.

While fishing on Lake Jackson one day in July, Bob Gates found the surface temperature nearly 90 degrees and decided he would have better luck casting plugs in the cooler waters of the Yellow River section. The river water was eight degrees cooler, and he caught three largemouth bass that struck a diving, vibrating Deep Wee-R plug.

His next strike felt like he'd hooked onto a pickup truck in second gear, and he discovered the fish had straightened the treble hooks. Suspecting it was a big striped bass, he tied on a bigger plug, a Maxi-R, also a deep diver.

Fishing alone three and a half hours, Gates cast into holes 10 to 20 feet deep and found stripers lying in the cooler water. He caught nine stripers and kept his limit of six weighing a total of 51 lb. 4 oz., the largest going an ounce over ten pounds.

"I lost two-thirds of the fish that hit," he said. "They took two plugs away from me, and six hooks were straightened slap out. And, on some of the plugs the O-rings pulled out. Those stripers also pulled open the snaps tied on the end of my line. It was fantastic. When they hit the plugs, they didn't turn them loose. I hung two stripers that would have weighed 15 to 17 pounds apiece, and when I got them halfway back to the boat, they pulled the hooks out of the plugs."

Gates said that on the first run, the stripers would take 35 to 50 yards of line, and he had to turn on his bow-mounted electric motor and move into the center of the river to follow the fish.

Big Ones Feed at Night

Night fishing on reservoirs in the summer never has been my cup of tea. I begin to nod and doze about one-thirty or two o'clock, and it's a wonder a fat, old bass hasn't stolen my rod and reel after swallowing the plastic worm.

Frankly, the very thought of fishing at night in the late autumn or early winter is enough to make me shiver and put another log on the fire. Some fishermen give it a try, though, and they put big'uns in their boats.

Between October and the end of December, a number of Georgia anglers enjoy terrific success fishing at night for striped bass with saltwater-size plugs near the banks and boat docks on Lake Sinclair and Lake Lanier. With two or three persons fishing in a boat, the catches might total one to two hundred pounds in a single night during the periods when stripers were moving and actively feeding in the shallow areas.

"It was real good at night on Sinclair until mid-December," said Les Ager of Fort Valley, Georgia, a state fisheries biologist who has done a great deal of work in the striper program.

"They were casting Model A's in the Tennessee shad, bone-and-white patterns. When the water got colder, they switched to the Sassy Shad and Burke Shimmy Shad lures."

Striped bass, generally running in the 2- to 12-pound class, moved close to the Lake Sinclair banks, onto shallow points, and near boat docks at night to feed on threadfin shad, their favorite forage. On Lake Lanier, the stripers also were found feeding in the shallows, but fishermen cast much bigger artificial lures.

"We caught stripers on big plugs in Lanier—the Cordell Redfin and five- to seven-inch Rebels," said Ager. "The lure color didn't seem to matter. Stripers weighing 12 to 30 pounds each were caught at night on Lanier. Some were topwater strikes, too. You set the hook and see the fish breaking at the top. I've used 12- to 20-pound test line."

One night, the biologist and his companion boated nine striped bass that averaged 15 pounds.

"On a typical night, you might fish from sundown until one-thirty or two in the morning," said Ager. "You might get five or six strikes, and, if lucky, you'd get one or two stripers in the boat. Usually you'd get only one fish in a spot and have to move."

After Lanier's surface temperatures dropped to 46 to 48 degrees, the stripers sharply cut down on their feeding activity, and Ager told me their food requirements would not increase until water temperatures began rising in the early spring.

Tracking the Stripers

Fishermen who have experienced fights with rugged, long-running striped bass are generous with their words of praise for the great game fish, but frequently they are frustrated in their efforts to locate them in a reservoir. I am reminded of the late Connie Mack, who managed the Philadelphia Athletics many years and once observed that pitching was 75 percent of baseball. If Mr. Mack had been an angler, he might have concluded that the ability to locate the fish is over 75 percent of fishing. Anybody can accidentally stumble upon a fish, but the consistently successful angler has learned how to think like a fish and to locate the rascals without wasting a whole day.

Keenly aware of this factor in fishing, the Georgia Game and Fish Division did anglers a big favor by tracking the movement of striped bass in 15,330-acre Lake Sinclair on the Oconee River in central Georgia.

Fisheries biologist Les Ager of Fort Valley said that radio transmitters, half the size of a cigar, were surgically implanted in body cavities of striped bass that weighed between 3 and 17 pounds. A different frequency was assigned to each of several fish, and radio signals were monitored by fisheries teams each week.

The range of the radio signal was ½ mile, and the life of the batteries was an average of four months.

"This has shown us two important things about striped bass," said Ager. "Water temperature and current attract stripers. In the summer, when water temperatures are hot in a reservoir, striped bass, despite everything, will seek out cooler temperatures, even if it means doing without satisfactory oxygen or food."

Hundreds of striped bass spent the summer in Shoulderbone Creek, which empties into the Oconee River in the upper reaches of Lake Sinclair, only a short distance below the Wallace Dam on Lake Oconee.

"Fishermen were catching plenty of stripers in that creek all summer," said Ager. "We used an electric shocker in population studies and found nothing but stripers. There was almost nothing for the striped bass to eat in Shoulderbone Creek, and they were in poor condition, but they stayed because the creek was 10 degrees cooler than the rest of Lake Sinclair."

Fishermen watching their depth finders would see the screens light up like a Christmas tree with numerous orange blips when their boats passed over deep holes where stripers had congregated.

"I have talked to people in Florida, Tennessee, and Oklahoma, and they have seen the same thing happen with stripers," said Ager. "The old-time river fishermen would have told you years ago that you find stripers in holes in rivers and in cooler springs in the summer."

Many striped bass also lingered for weeks in the dredge channel and tailrace below the Wallace dam, attracted by the current of the water passing through the gates from Lake Oconee. Stripers favored the areas with current and identical conditions above and below Lake Sinclair's dam, too. As Sinclair's surface temperatures grew colder in late November and December, the striped bass moved in large numbers into the vicinity of the Harlee Branch steam plant on Sinclair.

Water is pumped from Sinclair to cool the plant's power generating system, then discharged at higher temperatures back into the lake. This causes the stripers to join other species of game fish and pan fish in the area. Ager said stripers also were found in the current where the water was being pumped and in the discharge area, the warm water cove.

Why does current attract the striped bass?

"This is a mystery," the fisheries biologists say, pointing out that the striped bass is a saltwater species that had been stocked in freshwater lakes. "It could be the genetic makeup, and they associate with currents and tidal flow in the ocean."

One rather surprising discovery in the monitoring program was that many of the striped bass did not move as far as previously believed.

"Our weekly monitoring revealed," Ager said, "that one of the stripers stayed within ½ to ¾ of a mile of the Lake Sinclair dam for five months. Another fish has been in Island Creek for two months, and he has stayed within 50 to 100 yards of the same location."

A striper that was tagged and released in the tailwaters of the Lake Oconee dam traveled down the Oconee River to the warm-water cove at the steam plant on Lake Sinclair, remaining there in the late autumn.

Striper Honeymoon

Striped bass don't send their sweethearts cards, flowers, or candy on Valentine's Day, but they become quite romantic in their fashion in February. This is the time of the year when stripers from the Atlantic Ocean hit the road—a river of their own choosing—on a long journey that some fishermen might liken to a honeymoon.

In the late winter and very early spring when water temperatures are in the low 50s, the striped bass begin spawning runs far up Georgia rivers, coinciding with trips by shad along the same routes.

Clint Harper, operator of Two Way Fishing Camp on the Altamaha River near Darien, Georgia, said fishermen enjoy action with shad and stripers at least until the end of March.

"They'll catch stripers weighing from a few pounds to 18 pounds or more," he said. "There are some much bigger stripers that are hooked, but they break off or take all the line off a reel. A friend of mine saw some fish boiling on the surface in a creek, and he said one of 'em must have weighed close to 50 pounds."

On the stripers' spawning runs, a variety of artificial lures, even plastic worms, will draw strikes. It's not unusual for an angler casting a shad-like plug to hook something he cannot possibly turn, and he helplessly watches 100 yards of line stripped from his reel's spool.

A fisherman from nearby Brunswick, Vernon Alston, likes to

head up the Altamaha River in his small johnboat and troll for striped bass. He uses a 9.8 horsepower outboard motor to reach the productive stretches of water, so fishing isn't an expensive pastime for him.

"I use a Mitchell 300 [spinning reel], ten-pound monofilament line and a blue-and-silver, broken-back Rebel or a broken-back Rapala," he said. "If I'm fishing for largemouth bass, I usually fill my spool with eight-pound line."

Jointed lures in the black-and-silver, black-and-gold, red-and-white, and the silver flash patterns also are productive in striper fishing.

"I start trolling 200 yards below the mouth of my favorite creek and pass over some logs," said Alston. "In fact, I get largemouths at the same time I'm trolling for stripers. The bigmouth bass go up to three or four pounds, and I catch stripers weighing six to ten pounds. The strike—it's like a piece of dynamite. I'll tell you, the striped bass is the most dynamite fish you ever had hold of with light tackle."

His open-face spinning reel's drag is set so that a striper will have to exert at least six pounds of pressure to take any line off the spool. Ten-pound monofilament line is sufficient on a spinner with that setting, and a big fish slowly will be worn out, Alston said.

"You can stop a 150-pound man with fishing line tied to a harness on his back in less than one hundred yards with ten-pound monofilament and a reel's drag set at six pounds of pressure," he said. "If you tried to swim straight away from me, I would wear you out. You'd start turning right or left. Once you turn, I've got you."

When Alston or his fishing partner gets a strike from a striper in the river, he cuts off the motor, and they anchor the johnboat and begin casting lures in hopes a school of fish is in the vicinity.

Lower reaches of the Altamaha River are affected by the rise and fall of the Atlantic's tides.

"The tide makes a difference in our fishing," said Alston. "It's best on the outgoing tide from the top when it begins to run off and then down to half-tide. Then the fishing, if you're trolling, begins to slow down. People fishing with shrimp under floats keep getting strikes, though."

Trolling for Trophies

Trolling is a very easy and productive way to fish for striped bass. Many anglers on the southern impoundments use electronic depth finders or the more expensive chart recorders to locate favorable habitat such as rocky ledges, creek and river channels and old banks, submerged timber and deep holes where the fish may be lying in the summer.

They troll through such areas with a deep running lure such as a Hellbender, Bomber, Water Dog, Rebel, or Jim Bagley's long-lipped balsa shad on the end of 17- to 25-pound test line. Either a spinning reel or a baitcasting reel will be satisfactory, but it must have rather large line storage capacity on the spool and a strong, smooth drag mechanism.

Many fishermen prefer to fish with a double rig consisting of a three-way swivel, a deep-diving plug on a two- or three-foot piece of line, and another bait on a four- or five-foot line. The trailing bait on the longer line could be a spinning lure, wobbling silver spoon, a jig with hair or feathers, or a shad-like plug such as a ThinFin or a Hot Spot. The short-lip black-and-silver Rapala is another good choice for this rig.

A Georgia fishing friend told me about an angler on the Santee Cooper lakes who trolls all spring and summer for striped bass with a black-and-silver or a black-and-gold, long-lipped Rebel. He likes the darker lure on a cloudy or drizzly day and the lighter pattern under a clear sky.

While trolling on a reservoir, an angler also is likely to pick up some white bass, largemouth and spotted bass and perhaps a walleye.

Spooning in Winter

During the winter, striped bass are hooked at depths ranging from 25 to 60 feet by fishermen vertically jigging spoons on ledges, edges of creek channels, brushy submerged islands, and standing timber.

Fluttering spoons that resemble crippled or dying shad and weigh ⅓ to ½ ounce can be quite effective. While fishing especially deep water, however, you will find that they flutter too slowly to the bottom, and your bait won't be lying directly beneath the boat in the brushy area or on the dropoff that you spotted on the depth finder. Many fishermen prefer spoons that weigh ¾ of an ounce or a full ounce and are designed for a quicker, straighter fall.

Lead slab spoons such as Tom Mann's Mann-O-Lure and Jim Bagley's Salty Dog Spoon are fine baits for deep jigging. Favorite spoons on deep, relatively clear lakes include the Sidewinder, Hopkins Shorty, and Little Cleo. Mepps offers a glittering spoon, the Striper Killer, which flutters down with a tantalizing action like a dying shad in that frigid water. Mann's Little George, a tailspinner with a lead body, also is a good striper bait that can be vertically jigged, hopped across the bottom or cast and retrieved with sharp twitches of the rod tip.

VII

White Bass

Charles Salter (left) and Eddie Withrow had good reasons to smile after landing this string of white bass that struck small artificial lures in the spawning run up a river in the spring.

Give Them a High Grade

During the past 20 years or more, white bass have been introduced in reservoirs constructed in southern states by power companies and the U.S. Army Corps of Engineers.

The handsome white fish with black stripes along its sides, a high dorsal fin, broad tail, and an arched back has become one of the favorite game fish among the beginning fishermen, the veteran anglers, the young and the old.

White bass can be caught in any month of the year in the Deep-South impoundments, but it is in the spring when they head up rivers on their spawning runs that the action really gets fast and furious.

When water temperatures reach about 52 degrees in the rivers that feed into the big lakes, white bass feel the instinct to spawn and begin leaving the "flat water" and heading upstream. Male white bass start the spawning journey first, soon followed by the females heavily laden with eggs.

The male and female white bass usually congregate in extremely large numbers in shoal areas on the rivers, where reproduction occurs and the tiny eggs with an adhesive quality adhere to roots, limbs, submerged trees, and stumps. After the spawning ritual is completed, the fish begin their long trip back down the river to the big water.

When word spreads that white bass are starting their spawning runs, fishermen begin a mad dash by the hundreds to their favorite rivers, and they spend hours searching for the fish by casting or trolling a variety of artificial lures. Many of them use electronic gadgets—flasher-type depth finders and the more expensive chart recorders. The recorder produces a graph showing the contours of the river bottom and gray marks indicating the presence of fish—sometimes large schools.

Anglers cast in hopes of locating white bass lying extremely close to the banks. Little spinning lures with silver or gold blades and also small shad-like crankbaits are productive, as are white or yellow lead-head hair jigs and small silver spoons.

Those choosing to troll sometimes use a double rig with a three-way swivel. The main line is tied to one ring on the swivel, and a deep-diving plug such as a Hellbender, Bomber, or Rebel is tied to a two- or three-foot line on the second ring. The fisherman usually ties a spinning lure, spoon, or small jig to a longer piece of line on the third ring.

It's not uncommon for a fisherman to enjoy a "double" if he pulls his rig through a large concentration of white bass on the spawning run that are in the mood to strike the imitation minnows.

During the summer, the white bass spend much of their time in the deeper, cooler water, but early in the morning and late in the afternoon they often rise to the surface and attack schools of threadfin shad, their favorite forage. On a calm day when a lake's surface is as slick as a mirror, the school of white bass feeding on the surface can be seen from a considerable distance. To be prepared for this "jump fishing," a wise angler keeps a silver spoon or a tail-spinner, such as the Little George, on his extra rod and reel.

The school of white bass may stay on top of the water only a couple of minutes, then go back down, only to reappear moments later more than a cast's distance behind or way ahead of your boat. Sometimes fishermen are able to remain with the school and can catch enough white bass for many enjoyable suppers back home.

During the winter months, the white bass stay in deep water, feeding less frequently because the cold temperatures have sharply lowered their metabolism. Although the white bass in winter are much less active, they still occasionally can be taken on silver spoons that are jigged vertically next to a boat over standing timber, brush piles, rocky dropoffs, and submerged islands.

On March 8, 1972, on California's Ferguson Lake, Norman W. Mize used a Mepps Spinner to catch a world record 5 lb. 5 oz. white bass. The record was broken again March 31, 1977, when David S. Cordill caught a 5 lb. 9 oz. white bass in the Colorado River, Texas.

Did a World Record Shrink?

Sometimes Jeff Hobbins looks at the beautiful, mounted white bass on a wall in his Decatur, Georgia, home and feels mixed emotions, considering what might have been.

He is very proud to know that the 5 lb. 1 oz. white bass was accepted as a Georgia state record. But Jeff looks at that fish and says, "I had a world record fish in Lanier in 1971. There was not any doubt about it."

Jeff told me that his white bass was not put on the scales until it spent nearly two days in an ice chest without ice or water. When a fish dries out, the loss of body moisture results sometimes in a decrease of several ounces in actual weight.

At that time the world record for white bass was 5 lb. 4 oz.

On the night of June 16, 1971, Jeff Hobbins and Tyre Watson of Decatur were fishing with threadfin shad for rainbow trout in the mouth of a creek on 38,000-acre Lake Lanier.

"My partner and I used a depth finder and found the fish on a dropoff where we usually fish in Lake Lanier," he said. "I guess it is about 40 feet deep, and there is a ledge. We usually catch big white bass there late in the year, also big trout.

"On the same trip we caught the big white bass, we had two rainbows that weighed seven pounds each. The fish came through there where two creeks meet. They seem to hit live bait better than plugs."

He was fishing with a No. 2 hook with a big slip sinker and a shad minnow, allowing the boat to drift slowly in the wind.

"I actually thought it was a big trout until it made its first run and didn't jump," Jeff said. "Then I figured it must be a big white bass."

It took several minutes for him to pull the fish out of deep water with his ultra-light spinning reel, light action 6½-foot rod and four-pound test line.

"A good white bass makes strong runs and really fights hard," he said. "He reminds me of the jack crevalle. I think a white will out-fight a largemouth day in and day out."

He and his fishing partner used to fish frequently for white bass in the Chestatee and Chattahoochee rivers, both of which flow into Lanier, but each spring when the whites were on their spawning runs, the streams were very crowded with boats from all over north Georgia.

"We decided we'd do better fishing for whites in the lake early in the summer. I have found that bigger white bass are caught in the lake than in the rivers."

Leon Kirkland, now director of the Georgia Game and Fish Division but at that time chief of its fisheries division, told me, "If that white bass [caught by Jeff Hobbins] had eaten one more mess of shad, it would have been a world record. I believe there's an excellent possibility someone will catch a world record white bass in Lake Lanier. If that fish had lived another six months, it would have broken the record."

On several occasions, Eddie Withrow of Lula, Georgia, a bus driver, and I have caught big strings of white bass on Lake Lanier. I remember one cold, wet, miserable day in the early spring when we cast deep-diving purple Rebels and caught a big mess of whites, the six largest being females that weighed 3 lb. to 3 lb. 10 oz. each.

Twice in my life I have had the pleasure of boating white bass weighing exactly four pounds. I hooked the first one while trolling a long, deep-diving, black-and-purple Rebel in the

Chattahoochee River arm of Lanier on a cool and windy day in late March, 1969.

The second four-pounder was in a big school of white bass that had cornered threadfin shad in a feeding frenzy between a log and a point in a cove off the Chattahoochee in the upper end of Lanier.

My fishing partner, J. L. "Junior" Collis, and I were fishing with plastic worms for black bass when the whites suddenly began thrashing on the surface and attacking the shad. Each of us had a lure on an extra rod and reel, and we went to work on the rascals immediately.

We stayed with them for half an hour, catching 25 white bass that weighed a total of 55 pounds. My four-pounder was the largest fish. However, Junior pulled one within several feet of the boat that might have been pretty close to the world record, but the hook tore out of its lip.

The lures that we used in that frantic period of great action were a Cordell white jig with white soft plastic grub tail, a Little George, and a deep-diving black-and-purple Rebel.

Several white bass would chase a lure at the same time, and when one grabbed the bait, three or four others would follow it to the boat. I saw a big white bass following closely behind my Little George, and I stopped retrieving with about four feet of line off the rod tip and began a figure-eight motion right beside the boat. The three-pound white bass struck and I set the hook, raised the rod tip high and swung the fish over into the boat.

Hitting the Bullseye

In April, 1969, Tom McMullan and I rode in his small boat up the Chattahoochee, stopping within casting distance of the shoals, where a fantastic number of white bass had gathered to spawn. Dogwoods and pink wildflowers had blossomed on the river's steep banks, making us suspect our timing was right and that water temperatures were sufficiently warm to attract the romantic fish.

"Some people think the white bass have quit running in the Chattahoochee," said Tom. "I believe they're here. We'll try it and, if we don't get 'em, we'll head on up to the shoals."

We began casting Mepps Spinners with No. 2 silver blades as close as possible to the fallen trees, logs, and rocks, also under branches reaching out from the brushy shore. Sometimes the boat was anchored within easy casting range of the bank; other times we let it drift slowly in the current.

Moving frequently in search of white bass, we worked the shoreline thoroughly, and soon began catching some young fish, which felt like tough oldtimers in the current. Every strike came very close to the bank.

The white bass grabbing the little spinners weighed 1 to 1½ pounds, but they were rugged fighters, making a dash toward tree tops or racing into deeper, faster water that they used to great advantage.

Our catch totaled 25 fish when we stopped for lunch, and I

figured we had done pretty well for the day, but the best was yet to come. Early in the afternoon we drifted back down the Chattahoochee and tangled with a few more scrappy white bass, some going two pounds each.

Once, when my lure was caught on a snag next to the bank, I leaned over the bow to get it and counted six white bass only two feet from the boat. I was tempted to jump into the river and grab them.

Three other boats were anchored in a 60-yard stretch of the river when we stopped at one of Tom's favorite spots, a fallen tree which apparently was a white bass subdivision during the spawning period.

His first cast to a little place between the tree trunk and a branch produced a two-pounder, and the second throw was good for another nice size fish. The third cast fooled a three-pound white bass, and the fourth earned him one of equal size. Tom hooked a 3½-pound white bass on his fifth cast.

Fishing with a small spinning reel, light line, and a limber rod, he was enjoying every ounce of those fish. He held on for dear life and slowly but surely wore them to a frazzle.

Tom landed another big one on his sixth cast, and at that point I concluded the fish were throwing a party at that single address and leaving other "houses" empty. Continuing this amazing streak, Tom caught nine big white bass, the largest weighing 3¾ pounds, on ten casts.

Late in the afternoon, we pulled up the anchor and headed back to the boat launching ramp with a total catch of 55 white bass and one bluegill.

Pass the Minnows, Please

White bass in Georgia's Oconee River probably have been warning their children and grandchildren about D. P. Belcher for many years. Just the mere mention of this man from Madison, Georgia, is enough to make the white fish with black stripes on their sides flip their fins in fear.

The retired dairy inspector grinned and admitted that his fishing technique on the river is a little bit different from the methods used by some other fishermen.

"I'm an outlaw on the white bass fishing," said Belcher, as a gray cat jumped into his lap in the den of his home in Madison. "I don't fish for them like the other boys.

"I use a barrel swivel with a No. 4 hook. The hook is 12 to 14 inches below the swivel, with a lead pinched onto the line between the swivel and the hook."

This rig permits him to avoid line twist, and he prefers a No. 4 Aberdeen hook because if it becomes snagged on the river bottom, he can straighten it and save his terminal tackle. The selection of live bait is a key to his success, too.

"I use branch minnows," said Belcher. "White bass hit them decidedly better than other minnows."

When white bass travel upstream in the spring on their spawning run, Belcher anchors his boat next to a deep hole near the shoals in the Oconee River above Lake Sinclair.

"You flip the bait crossways of the current, and that lead

bounces on the bottom," he explained. "The current brings it on around, and you bring it on around and cast again."

One day in early April, Belcher and a Madison friend, Charles Cunningham, pulled their limits of white bass out of one hole; the fish averaged 1½ pounds.

"The fish are lying in that deep water some days," said Belcher. "But sometimes they are not there. They're in that ripple. You can also catch 'em with a Rapala or a lead-head, white-feather jig."

How does he know the white bass will be in a particular hole in the river?

Belcher, who knows some sections of the river like the palms of his hands, said, "The white bass will come up and strike the minnows every now and then. They will boil up on the surface. You more or less have got to know the river bottom. It's highly important, whether you're fishing a farm pond, this river, or Lake Lanier, to know the bottom."

April Fever for White Bass

Each spring since the early 1960s, Earl Palmer has been hooked on white bass in Georgia's Lake Sidney Lanier. The magnificent, piscatorial obsession returns with its customary intensity when the Chattahoochee River arm of the lake reaches about 52 degrees on the surface.

Earl, a salesman who was raised in Cleveland, Georgia, only a short ride north of his Gainesville home, is aware that the rise in water temperatures gives the white bass the signal to think of romance and swim upstream.

"Around the first of April, they're really in the river," he said. "When I say river, I'm talking about the area above Lula bridge. Below the bridge, it's the lake. The peak of the white bass spawning run is about the first two weeks of April. It depends on the weather, the water temperature, and rain."

Early in May, he has boated white bass five or six miles above the popular shoals. A johnboat would be a necessity in that stretch of water.

His biggest catch in one day was a limit of 30 white bass weighing a total of more than 50 pounds.

"One day I was casting a Rebel Super R plug on a point where a guy three days earlier had caught three largemouth bass weighing a total of 21 pounds," he said. "The first fish hit and it was tearing line off my reel. It was a white, and I threw it in the live well. I cast again and hooked another one. On five casts I caught five white bass, and they weighed 21 pounds."

One of his favorite lures for white bass is a marabou or bucktail jig, preferably white. Earl makes a white spinnerbait, the open safety-pin-type of bait, which also is mighty deadly.

"It's got a ½-ounce head, a No. 4 silver blade and white bucktail or marabou feathers, tied on a one-ought-size hook," he said. "In the river, you can get up there in the current and chunk it to the banks around brush and logs, and it won't hang up like a jig. Lots of times the whites get in the river, and a cold front comes along, and they go to the center of the channel and drop down to the gravel bars and sand and hold. I let the spinnerbait swing with the current across the gravel bar."

In slack water back on the main part of the lake, Earl favors a Deep Wee-R with a black back and silver sides. Other effective baits in his arsenal are the Countdown Rapala, Bomber Model-A, small Big-O, Humpback Rebel, half-ounce Hot Spot, Little Cleo, and Little George.

Earl emphasized the importance of pin-point casting accuracy when the white bass are up in the river in April, because they frequently are found lying extremely close to the banks.

Usually he fishes for whites with an ultra-light spinning reel and six-pound line, which enable him to appreciate every ounce of those scrappy rascals.

"A good place to find white bass in the spring is an area where a feeder spring comes into the river or in a ditch or a wet-weather gully," he said. "They'll congregate around the mouth of a creek. I like to fish on a cloudy day."

The white bass spawning runs are somewhat cyclic, said Earl, observing that an excellent spring harvest of fish will be followed by two or three lean or only fair seasons.

"For a few minutes, a white bass is tough," he said, "but he gives up quicker than a largemouth. He doesn't have the stamina, and you don't get the top-water show. In the wintertime they are about equal in that cold water."

On Lake Lanier in the summer, Earl likes jump fishing for

white bass. The fish go into a feeding frenzy and attack a school of threadfin shad on the surface.

"I would throw a Little Cleo spoon first at the feeding white bass," he said. "Then I would use a Little George. I have done well with a top-water plug, a Heddon Tiny Torpedo. If I find a school of white bass on the surface, I rig two rods, one with a lure to throw at them and one with a plug to drop into them."

VIII
Walleye

Fair Fighter, Delicious Dinner

Some of us who grew up in the Deep South, fishing in warm, sluggish rivers and shallow lakes, weren't acquainted with the walleye. A high-school friend in Waycross in southeast Georgia saw a photograph of a walleye in a fishing magazine and remarked, "That's a fish they catch way up North or in Canada."

On vacation trips with their families to areas with higher elevations in the middle and upper South, some of these guys were surprised when they hooked walleyes while casting lures for largemouth or smallmouth bass.

The walleye, inhabiting cool, clear streams and reservoirs with sandy or gravel bottoms, still enjoys only a fraction of the popularity of the black bass, but it nevertheless is an important game fish in the South, and its fans are increasing every year.

Blue Ridge reservoir, the beautiful, deep, cool, 3,320-acre lake on the Toccoa River in northeast Georgia, appears to have a very large population of walleyes, but relatively few anglers are fishing for them.

A few dedicated, knowledgeable anglers, however, are casting for them with a variety of lures in the spring and trolling quite deep to hook them in the summer.

Kim Primmer of Calhoun, Georgia, a fisheries biologist for the Georgia Game and Fish Division, is an angler who casts an artificial lure specifically with walleyes in mind.

In his spare time in March several years ago, Primmer caught a number of walleyes while fishing in Blue Ridge for bass; of every ten fish that he boated, seven usually were bass and three were walleyes. That summer he picked up a few tips from local fishermen who were trolling deep-running plugs with success.

"When I really got into them was that December plugging right next to the bank," said Primmer. "I was casting the Rebel Wee Deep R that had a chartreuse side, orange belly and vertical black stripes, and I was fishing at night."

The average size walleye he landed was 14 or 15 inches long and weighed one pound or slightly more. His largest walleye weighed two pounds and was 19 inches long. The following spring he fished with minnows on the bottom, allowing his boat to drift in the wind, and he also cast to the banks with small, diving crankbaits in the bone or chartreuse patterns.

The largest member of the perch family, the walleye feeds mostly on little fish and crayfish. Among its numerous local names are walleyed pike, pike-perch, jack salmon, yellow pickerel, and blue pickerel. In northern rivers and lakes and in Canada, walleyes frequently are found in the two- to five-pound class, and it isn't uncommon for a seven- or eight-pounder to be taken.

Primmer admitted that the walleye isn't such a good fighter, but "when it comes to eating, it has them all beat."

"In December, I was cranking real slow, and sometimes the plug actually stopped close to the surface, and the walleyes came up and very gently took the plug," he said. "I would set the hook, and the fish would be there. There wouldn't be any fight. I just pulled them in."

He added, "Generally speaking, they take any kind of bait very gently, but every once in a while you get a rambunctious one that will really knock it."

During the summer weeks, he began using a trolling method that took lures down to a depth of 30 to 40 feet. He trolled with a plexiglass diving plane called the Pink Lady.

"It was kind of like a sheet of paper four inches by six inches, and underneath was a lead weight, and it tips forward in a diving position," said Primmer. "You pull it through the water bringing the line down, and when a fish hits, it trips it and pulls its nose up, causing it to plane back toward the surface.

"You attach the lure with a three- or four-foot leader behind it. The diving plane does nothing more than take it under the water. On the back end of the plexiglass there is attached a snap swivel with eight- to ten-pound leader."

Some northeast Georgia anglers troll an artificial lure that has a green back, silver sides, and yellow belly. Others prefer small, diving, vibrating plugs with blue backs and silver sides.

During the summer, when lakes have become quite warm and fish are discouraged from venturing into the shallows, it is important to remember to fish deep enough to reach levels where walleyes are comfortable. And use a good imitation of a minnow that has a little bit of wobble in its action, the biologist said.

"Most of this deep trolling in the summer is a lot of riding and a little bit of catching," he said. "Get a depth finder and follow the contour and get the bait down close to the bottom at a slow speed."

Some of the walleyes that were caught in the summer in Blue Ridge were lying at depths of 40 feet or more. One of the largest was a nine-pounder.

Walleyes are caught in greatest numbers during the early spring when they feel the instinct to spawn and move into shallow areas with sandy or gravel bottoms with water temperatures in the high 40s or 50s. At that point, the water would be 15 or more degrees too cold for a largemouth bass to give any thoughts to romance.

Action with little jigs, spinners, and crankbaits starts picking up in late February in the mountain streams.

One day in February shortly after Willis H. "Totsie" Wilbanks and Thomas Johnson of Jefferson, Georgia, stopped for lunch on the Tugaloo River near Toccoa in northeast Georgia, they saw a boat with two men drift around a bend.

Wilbanks told me he watched one of the men catch a walleye on a Doll Fly, a lead-head jig, and he decided it was high time to get his lure back in the water. The two Jefferson anglers rode upstream a short distance, cut off their outboard motor and began drifting.

Moments later Wilbanks cast a yellow diving lure next to a fallen tree beside the bank where he had seen a fish strike. He started his retrieve and suddenly felt a hard strike from a fish, which stayed close to the bottom, then made a short run and cut under the boat.

"My partner tied up to a snag, and I kept working the fish easily and finally got him to the top and saw it was a big walleye," said Wilbanks. "I told Johnson to get the net and he said we'd never get the fish in it."

Johnson managed to get the walleye's head into the net, with the tail hanging out, and lifted it over the side of the boat.

"The walleye flopped and I grabbed him," said Wilbanks. "One of the fingers on my left hand got in his mouth, and he bit it. He nailed me hard, too. It started bleeding, and I was so excited I didn't care."

The walleye weighed 9 lb. 5 oz. and was 28¼ inches long with a girth of 17 inches; local anglers described it as the largest ever landed in the Tugaloo River.

At that time, Georgia's state record walleye was the 11-pounder pulled out of Lake Burton April 13, 1963, by Steven Kenny of Atlanta. Leon Kirkland, then chief of fisheries for the state Game and Fish Division, told me Wilbanks's walleye from the Tugaloo River was believed to be the second biggest ever caught in the Peach State.

A world record 25-pound walleye was caught in Tennessee's Old Hickory Lake in August, 1960.

During the autumn and winter, anglers jigging spoons in deep water in Georgia's Lake Sidney Lanier and in Lake Hartwell on the Georgia and South Carolina border sometimes hook one- to four-pound walleyes. In most instances, the appearance of the critter with the bulging eyes is quite a surprise, because these folks braving the frigid temperatures are dyed-in-the wool bass fishermen.

However, if they pan-fry the walleye or add butter and lemon juice or white wine and bake it in an oven, they would have to admit the walleye is one of the most delicious fish found in America's lakes and rivers.

IX
Shellcracker

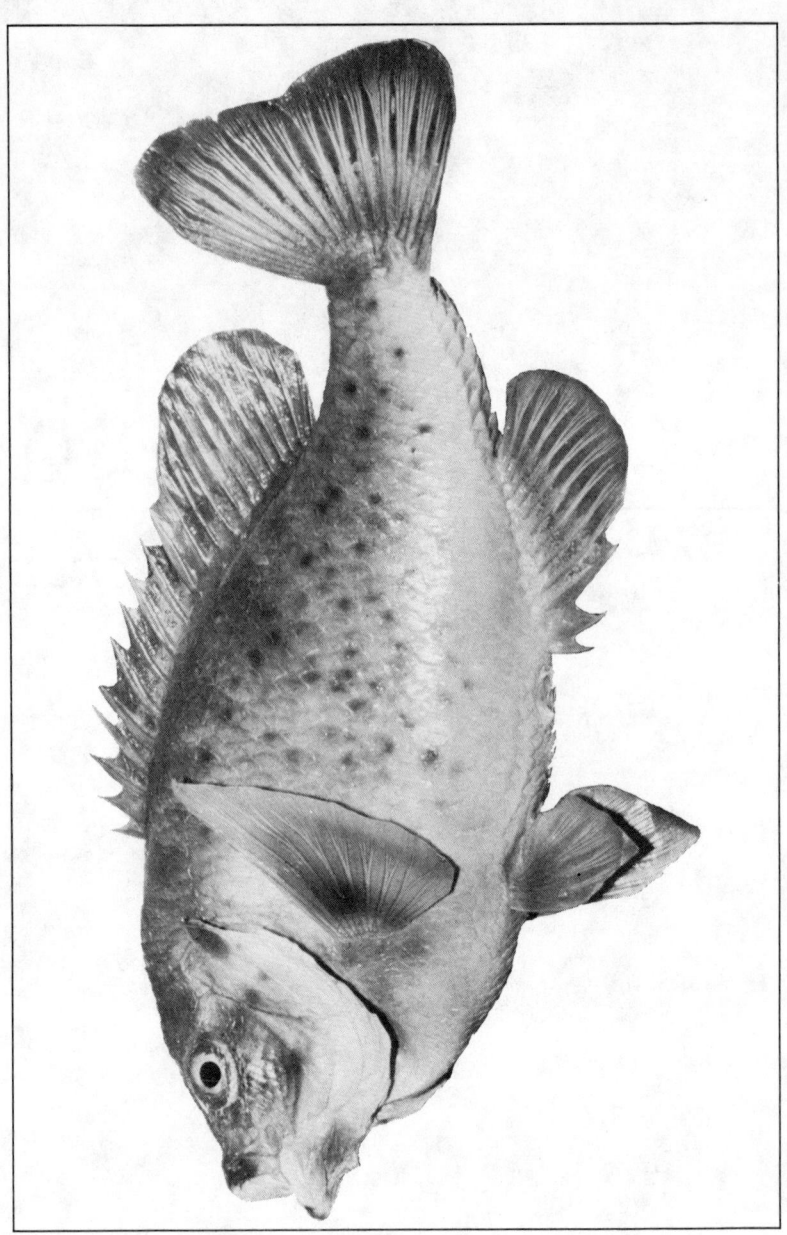

This 2-pound shellcracker was pulled out of a clear spring-fed lake on a sizzling day in July by Ike Williams, who likes to fish with long, limber fiberglass poles and bait his hooks with pink worms or crickets.

Real Pole-Benders

The redear sunfish, far better known among the folks in the cane-pole-and-spinner brigade as the "shellcracker," qualifies to be in the same major league with the bluegill as a mighty rugged fighter and a very delicious pan fish.

They are widely distributed in lakes and rivers across the South, and are commonly stocked along with bluegills and largemouth bass, in small ponds.

Fisheries biologists recommend that a new pond, which the owner intends to fertilize regularly, be stocked with 200 shellcrackers per acre, along with the usual 800 bluegills, 100 largemouth bass and, if desired, 100 channel catfish.

A fisheries biologist told me that shellcrackers are not nearly as prolific as bluegills, and, although they continue to reproduce for the first several years after a pond is stocked, they have been known in some instances to virtually disappear by the time the pond is seven or eight years old.

I have been told that the shellcracker sometimes will cross-breed with bluegills in small lakes. Over the years, several friends and I have caught pan fish which indeed did exhibit physical characteristics of these two species.

The body of the fish is olive and yellow with dark blotches, and five to ten dark bars run vertically on its sides. The male has a red spot on the tip of its gill flap, while the female has an orange spot.

Fishermen sometimes confuse the shellcracker with a pumpkinseed or a bluegill. On a Georgia pond, my fishing partner pulled out one and smiled and remarked, "That's a mighty pretty bluegill." I told him that it was a shellcracker, but he didn't believe me.

"Stick your little finger deep in his throat and tell me what you feel," I suggested.

In a moment my friend responded, "Ouch."

The shellcracker earned his nickname with the tooth-like structure deep in his throat that he uses to grind snails and other favored crustaceans found while grocery shopping in lakes and rivers.

Fortunately, my fishing partner's finger was just pinched a bit; I think he was impressed, though, with the difference between a shellcracker and a bluegill.

As a general rule, the shellcracker doesn't seem to be as attracted by insects as its sunfish cousin, the bluegill, and fishermen use such bait as red wigglers or Louisiana pinks. Occasionally they are caught on slowly sinking sponge bugs or little popping bugs.

While walking along the bank of a small pond and casting with an ultra-light spinning reel, I have caught a lot of shellcrackers with little spinners such as the Mepps and the Rooster Tail with "O" size silver or gold blades.

The same small lures can be productive when you troll very slowly across a pond with an electric motor. In the midst of a heat wave and dry spell in the summer, an angler can stand on the dam of a small pond, make a long cast, and allow the spinner to sink nearly to the bottom before beginning a slow retrieve with occasional pauses and twitches of the rod tip, and a shellcracker will grab it.

One afternoon in the late summer, I was fishing for bass in deep water next to a pond's dam, and something kept tap-tapping my six-inch blue plastic worm with a red tail, but I couldn't hook the rascal. I pinched off an inch of the worm at the head, and again there was a little tap, tap of a bite but no fish.

I shortened the plastic worm to barely 3½ inches, and when the fish bumped the bait again, I set the hook and got him. It was a handsome shellcracker that weighed nearly one pound.

This kind of teasing bite has occurred numerous times in other small ponds and also in reservoirs when I was bass fishing with six-inch blue or purple plastic worms with red tails, and I strongly suspect they were shellcrackers or bluegills.

Shellcrackers are easiest to catch along the shallow edges and in upper ends of farm ponds or on shallow flats of south Georgia and Florida lakes in the spring and early summer when they fan out nests to spawn after the water temperature has reached 70 to 75 degrees.

I asked Ike Williams, who lives near Atlanta but was reared in south Georgia, if he could tell the difference between the odor of bluegill and shellcracker beds. He has fished in Lake Blackshear and Georgia ponds and rivers since he was old enough to dig up an earthworm and hold a cane pole.

Ike laughed and said, "Well, you can't make much distinction. Have you ever smelled an over-ripe watermelon? If you have, you know what those bluegill and shellcracker beds smell like."

Did the scent also remind him of a musty basement?

"To a degree, maybe," he said. "But, it really is a sweetish smell. I can remember one day fishing on Lake Blackshear, near Cordele, Georgia, when the wind was blowing a little, and we could smell shellcracker beds.

"They usually bed in shallower water than bluegills, so I figured it was shellcrackers. My fishing partner and I hunted those beds almost two hours before we finally found them. We put 100 shellcrackers in the boat in an hour and a half. They bit red worms."

A shellcracker weighing 1 to 1½ pounds is pretty good bragging-size, but it's not uncommon to hear reports of 2-pounders being taken in southern farm ponds. Two pounds, 12 ounces was the biggest reported caught in Georgia for a number of years.

In north and central Florida lakes, fishermen have boated shellcrackers in the 2¾- to 3-pound class when the fish were spawning in the spring.

Sixteen years ago I figured the record would go untouched for a while after a 2 lb. 15 oz. shellcracker was caught in a lake near Ponte Vedra Beach, Florida.

But, in 1970, I opened the mail at the office and almost fell out of my chair when I saw a photograph of a 4 lb. 8 oz. shellcracker that struck a little spinner, a Mepps Comet Mino, in a small pond close to Boydton, Virginia.

Landed by Gene Ball of Norfolk, the shellcracker was 16½ inches long and had a girth of 17 inches.

I'd almost give a week's salary to hook that fish's twin sister on six-pound test line, an ultra-light spinning reel and a 6½-foot rod with the action of a willow branch. What a freak of nature that fish must have been.

An old fishing pal who shares my respect for this species once told me, "He's certainly in the same league with a bluegill as a fighter. I have caught some shellcrackers that weighed 10, 12, or 15 ounces on a fly rod, and I had to handle them like they were two- or three-pound bass. They turn their sides to you and put up a whale of a battle, and they just don't know when to quit."

X
Jackfish

Ol' Chain Sides—A Real Battler

The chain pickerel, much better known among southern fishermen as the "jack" or "jackfish," is probably the most underrated game fish prowling swamps, lakes, and warm, slow-flowing rivers below the Mason-Dixon line. The jackfish simply has been too doggone busy gorging himself and killing anything that would fit in his teeth-lined jaws to take the time to hire a good press agent.

Ever since my first fishing trip to the Okefenokee Swamp in southeast Georgia when I was 14 years old, I have considered the jackfish to be a mighty exciting game fish. I don't believe that I'd be willing to lend a dollar to a fisherman who didn't feel at least a little bit of respect for Mr. and Mrs. Chain Sides.

The jackfish is strong enough to make a spinning reel's or a baitcasting reel's drag scream as he strips off yards of line—he doesn't quit fighting until you pull him out of the water. The acrobatics he displays when he leaps high and shakes his head in an attempt to throw an artificial lure will match that of the largemouth bass.

When a hooked jackfish takes his first look at the side of your boat, he goes absolutely berserk, quickly gets his second wind, and fights even more violently for his life. As an old fishing buddy said, "When the jack sees that boat, he just plain goes nuts, becomes a wild-eyed psycho."

Bait your hook with minnows or crayfish—in south Georgia

we prefer to call those shelled critters crawfish or crawdads—and when a jackfish strikes with the manners of a paid assassin, you may wonder if your cane pole will be able to withstand the punishment. A jackfish 14 to 30 inches long will put a mighty sharp bow in a fiberglass or a graphite fishing rod, too. Remember that Mr. Chain Sides is a natural-born killer who plays for keeps.

My first encounter with the jackfish took place in the 700-square-mile Okefenokee Swamp, Georgia's gorgeous "land of the trembling earth," whose dark waters empty into the St. Marys River and the Suwannee River.

Dad and I were casting surface lures, the Creek Chub Darters in the silver flash pattern, in the Suwannee Canal, an almost 11-mile-long ditch dug in the late 1800s in a vain attempt to drain the swamp so that workers could more easily reach cypress trees with their saws.

Jackfish were lying next to grass, stumps, cypress knees, and the big, Spanish-moss-draped cypress trees, waiting to ambush a minnow, baby warmouth perch, kindergarten age bass, or a small snake.

Some spots were so shallow that we could see the wake of the approaching fish, a sight that gave me goose bumps. Surface strikes were so sudden and vicious that my hair must have been standing at attention.

Occasionally a jack would strike short—in south Georgia that's called a "rise"—and seconds later he would pounce upon the lure, biting down so hard that his razor-sharp teeth left a familiar autograph. It's unbelievable what damage a jackfish can inflict upon a wooden plug, especially one made of balsa, and those teeth can easily cut braided or monofilament line. We frequently resorted to wire leaders to save the lures when we trolled or cast in the Okefenokee.

Those rascals were crazy about artificial lures in flashy, brightly-colored patterns; red, orange, and yellow were effective, and a combination of red and white was good.

In the Suwannee Canal near Folkston and also in Billy's Lake on the other side of the Okefenokee, close to Fargo, I enjoyed success trolling for jackfish with a Johnson silver spoon trailing a piece of split pork rind on its hook, a shallow-running Hawaiian Wiggler with yellow skirt, and a small spinning lure with a silver blade.

Another favorite in the 1950s and 1960s was a wooden, cigar-shaped bait with a metal lip designed for shallow retrieve; Pflueger called it a Pal-O-Mine. Swamp fishermen gave it a more colorful name.

Some of us couldn't imagine how a sober man could have painted the plug in such a wildly scrambled red, orange, and yellow pattern. I don't remember seeing two painted exactly alike. The nickname "Scrambled Egg" spread all over south Georgia and north Florida.

The Scrambled Egg had a tantalizing wiggle on a retrieve that drove jackfish and also largemouth bass out of their minds, and it was a better than average imitation of a crippled minnow on the surface.

Another very deadly and popular lure for jackfish was a fragile-looking spinner called the Pflueger Fluted Spoon. It had a nickel-and-red blade, and a treble hook on the end of the wire shaft was decorated with red, yellow, and white feathers.

The Fluted Spoon was entirely too light to cast without an added piece of lead, so we trolled it behind a small outboard motor or an electric motor, allowing it to pass close to brush, grass beds, trees, and stumps.

This little spinning lure was not only highly effective for jackfish in the Okefenokee, but it also drew plenty of strikes from black bass, bowfin, and even warmouth.

I also liked to cast or troll the Heddon Vamp in the rainbow finish. This was a wooden plug with a metal lip that made it run shallow, and, because of its size, you could expect the jackfish that struck to be a fully grown member of the Chain Sides family.

Dad and I caught a tremendous number of jackfish on a homemade trolling bait that consisted of a strip of pork rind, which was split two or three inches so that a twitch of the rod tip would make it resemble kicking legs, and several single-barb hooks tied with braided line. This lure was highly efficient in its fish-hooking quality, but it was a pain in the neck to remove those hooks from a jack's jaw as it squirmed and thrashed around in a johnboat.

Bait shops and sporting goods stores today carry a variety of spinning lures and spinnerbaits that will attract jackfish. I especially like a small spinnerbait with a nickel blade and a wiggling soft plastic grub—either white or yellow.

A white-tailed jig, worked slowly with twitches of the rod tip, will arouse Mr. Chain Sides, and he'll tear into a six- to eight-inch, black or purple soft plastic worm being retrieved in a swimming action to imitate an eel or little snake.

Back in the early 1960s, when I first began fishing on 37,500-acre Lake Seminole in southwest Georgia, I learned that fishing camp operator Jack Wingate was among the plug-chunkers who respected the jumping jacks.

"He's a moody and mean fish, and his temper is always on the surface," said Jack. "He will strike another fish because he's hungry, but many times he kills bait fish just for the joy of it. He's a good fighter. Yessirreee. He never quits."

Seminole has a rather big population of these long, slender, greenish-brown fish with dark chain-like markings on the sides, a dorsal fin rising only several inches from its forked tail, and a mouth filled with rows of very sharp teeth.

The jacks spawn in south Georgia and Florida in February and March.

"The Spring Creek and Fish Pond Drain areas of Seminole have a lot of jackfish," said the fishing camp operator. "In the winter they'll be in less than five feet of water, around the grass. You can run a spinnerbait slowly or real fast over the grass beds, and it'll produce fish."

A seven-pound jackfish that Wingate said "looked kind of like a muskie" was the biggest he has ever seen in Seminole; the lunker hit a yellow spinnerbait.

"You'd think their favorite food would be threadfin shad," said Wingate, "and the shad is a good diet for them. But jackfish thrive on bream and other pan fish. A four-pound jackfish can swallow a hand-size bream."

A white spinnerbait with a white skirt and nickel blade is perhaps the best winter lure for jackfish in Seminole; the same colored lure with a plastic grub on the hook is a more effective bass bait.

Plugs that resemble shad also draw attacks from jackfish, but they must be retrieved rapidly to keep them off the vegetation. Wingate agreed that most of the lures that prove productive in the Okefenokee would work equally well in Seminole's jackfish neighborhoods.

"In the coldest water in winter, jackfish drop off the top of those grass beds, and you have to zip that spinnerbait out to the edge of the grass, turn it loose and let it fall five or six feet," said Wingate.

"He's a great fighter. He never quits. Maybe it's his streamlined mouth, but even though he's got a lure in it, he can close it and not hurt himself with the water coming through it. He's got a little of the tarpon in him and jumps a lot."

One characteristic of the jackfish that excites Wingate is the way the rascal follows a lure nearly to the rod tip before viciously attacking it beside the boat. A rod tip can be snapped when the jackfish bores down and streaks under the boat and heads for deeper water.

"With his streamlined body, he can turn sideways to you and give you a terrific pull. The most I can remember is one going around my boat a time and a half. You don't get a much better fighter than that."

Wingate observed that Old Chain Sides also will take a notion to slam into an artificial lure that isn't working properly on the surface.

"A top-water plug can be coming back to you foul-hooked, stern foremost, erratic, not making any sense at all. I don't think a bass would hit it. And, all of a sudden a ripple will start up eight to ten feet from your lure, and the torpedo will explode right on it."

A jackfish will travel much farther to strike a plug than a black bass.

"You don't have to cast close to him to get a strike sometimes," said Wingate. "He'll travel eight or ten feet on the charge to hit. The old jackfish—he's really got character.

"He's a natural inland tarpon. He strikes like a ton of bricks hitting your plug, and he takes it and goes. I have seen a jackfish clear the water three feet from a plug and come down on top of it and swallow it whole.

"A jack really goes into a frenzy when he sees the boat. I reckon he knows there is danger there, or something shouldn't be there. He'll try to get the line in the upper plate in his mouth and cut it."

Wingate has observed over the years that the jackfish seem to strike best on a cloudy day. I can remember bright days in the Okefenokee or on Seminole when jacks would show little interest in our lures, but when the sun was behind a cloud a few moments, Mr. Chain Sides would nail the plug as if there were no tomorrow.

In Seminole the jointed (broken-back) lures in black-and-silver, black-and-gold, or black-and-purple patterns are productive baits when fishing for jacks. Another consistent producer of strikes is a silver spoon with a white or yellow skirt, and a spoon is also deadly with a strip of pork rind attached to the hook.

Wingate said that fishermen who refuse to bother with cleaning and cooking jackfish just don't realize what a treat they're missing.

"Most people don't want to mess with a jack, but he's the sweetest fish out there," he said. "He compares in eating quality with a four-finger bream or a shellcracker. They're bony, so we scale them and cut them into sections and gash them from the outside into the backbone, then fry them in deep fat in a skillet. When you gash a sucker from the inside to the outside before cooking it, the sucker has a similar taste to the jackfish."

A fisherman casting lures in jackfish territory would be wise to keep a good pair of pliers or a landing net within reach so that he can avoid injury to his hands when putting that wild critter in the boat. The rascal's extremely sharp teeth can seriously injure your hand; and if you don't hold his mouth with the pliers, he'll shake his head and sink a plug's treble hook in your hand or leg.

The world record jackfish weighed 9 lb. 6 oz., was 31 inches long and had a girth of 14 inches, and was caught in a south Georgia pond February 17, 1961, by Baxley McQuaig, Jr., of Homerville, who was casting a black Johnson spoon with pork rind.

That was indeed a jackfish of astonishing size, but in 1971, I learned that an even bigger one had managed to avoid angler's hooks and was found dead apparently of natural causes in Lake Worth on the Flint River near Albany.

Fisheries biologists Mike Gennings and Larry McSwain were conducting a study of the life history of spotted suckers when they saw what appeared from a distance to be a big bowfin or gar on the surface.

"I couldn't believe it when we got closer," said Gennings. "It was a big chain pickerel."

The huge chain pickerel, or jackfish, dead an estimated 24 hours, weighed 9 lb. 12 oz., and was 33 inches long. Gennings estimated that when alive in 2,500-acre Lake Worth, the fish would have weighed more than ten pounds.

"The fish probably died of natural causes," said Gennings. "We took a scale sample and determined that this chain pickerel was seven years old. This fish was a female and had a very flaccid stomach. It may have already spawned, which is not unheard of in south Georgia in January."

I was reminded that on other occasions, near-record fish had been found dead in forgotten or remote and seldom-fished bodies of water.

"I think there's a good possibility we have another record chain pickerel in a Georgia lake or river," said Gennings. "We have a good chance of breaking some other fishing records in this state."

XI
Catfish

E. H. Armor grins as he admires his favorite fish, a channel catfish, which bit a red wiggler in a farm pond. Armor recommends a catfish supper at least twice a week, explaining it's good brain food and helps increase a person's life expectancy.

You'll Live Longer

E. H. Armor of Greensboro, Georgia, was only six years old when he was introduced to channel catfish, and it definitely wasn't a case of love at first sight. He jumped from the front to the back seat of his father's car and stepped on a sack filled with catfish. The stiff spine of a catfish stuck through his big toe.

Armor grinned and recalled, "The doctor operated on me twice, and I never have gotten over it yet. My toe still hurts when I get around a catfish."

His father, Edgar Harvey Armor, began teaching him to catch creek and river catfish with baskets, trotlines, limb lines, and cane poles.

For 30 years the Greene County landowner has been raising channel catfish in small ponds on a farm near Greensboro and catching and selling them.

A week without two or three catfish suppers would be absolutely unbearable, in his estimation. If heaven contains any farm ponds, most will be stocked with channel catfish, Armor assured me.

He said, "The first night you're in heaven, the Lord will have his folks serve fried catfish and turnip greens."

Armor grinned and tried to convince me that a Biblical verse supports his belief that the catfish, whose body is covered by skin, is superior to scaled fish such as the bluegill, crappie, or bass.

Trying to suppress a smile, he said, "If you read the Bible fast, you see a lot of things. One verse says, 'The Lord maketh scale fish to be chopped up and fed to catfish.' I haven't found that verse in a revised version of the Bible, though."

Armor believes the Georgia General Assembly made a grievous error in choosing the largemouth bass as the official state fish instead of the bewhiskered, noble channel catfish.

He explained that a person would benefit greatly from eating catfish twice a week; the catfish provide important protein and essential "brain food," he said, and the meat increases one's life expectancy 12 percent.

Armor, a bachelor in his late 50s, said his married friends are convinced that catfish also has rejuvenating qualities.

Perhaps Armor should post a sign on his lake bank that says "Families that eat catfish together stay together."

On the dinner and supper table or at the end of a fishing line, the channel catfish is unequalled by any freshwater fish, says Armor, despite what you hear about rainbow trout, black bass, and bluegills.

"If you are fishing in a mountain creek with spider web on a small weed, like most say they do, trout are obliged to pull," said Armor. "Use a tiny rod and four-pound line, and a six-ounce trout is bound to bend it.

"You hook a bass, and he makes three or four runs. Hook a crappie, and he makes one surge and stops completely. A bream fights pretty well. But a channel catfish will fight you until you pull him out on the bank."

He is convinced that a channel catfish is stronger pound for pound than the largemouth or smallmouth bass.

"A catfish's eyes are on the bottom of his head, and he feeds down; and when he's hooked, he heads for the bottom. A bass's eyes are up, and he jumps, and you reel him closer to the bank. It's harder to pull something up from the bottom than from the top. A catfish pulls and goes down."

A catfish relies heavily upon its keen sense of smell to find food in the lakes and rivers. Fishermen use a wide variety of baits on their hooks to attract the cats' attention.

"I've caught catfish on chewing gum and soap," said Armor. "The most overrated bait is catalpa worms. The skin of a chicken neck is one of the best baits I've ever seen. I saw a man catch a 13¾-pound catfish on that skin."

Other very productive baits include small minnows, rotten oysters, shrimp, a piece of eel, a section of frog, chopped shad, chicken gizzard, chicken liver, wasp larva, earthworms, Louisiana pinks, red wigglers, and worms that feed on corn.

Catfish are primarily nocturnal feeders, but they also feed just after sunrise and for a period before sundown.

"The best time to go catfish fishing is right during and after a rainstorm," said Armor. "I had said it was because rain washes ants and bugs into the water. But Wayne Thomaston of the Game and Fish Department said it was the change in water temperatures that made them feed when it rains."

Armor tossed a handful of high-protein, pelleted commercial feed to channel catfish, which almost smiled as they rose to the surface and gulped it.

"I can catch catfish year-round, but January and February are the slowest months," he said. "Even in the winter, you can put out jugs with hooks baited with minnows, leave 'em two or three days, and sooner or later you are going to catch a catfish."

Years ago he occasionally baited his hooks with little pieces of soap, and the scent would attract catfish from a considerable distance.

Armor often fishes from the bank or a johnboat on one of his ponds with a closed-face reel and rod, his baited hook on the bottom. How does he know when to set the hook if a catfish bites and refuses to move?

"How do I know when to breathe?" he asked, grinning. "When the line gets tight, set the hook, rear back and holler. I have got another way to fish, too. See this cane pole? It has six lines and hooks, and I let it float in the water. You can tell when the catfish bites, because the pole starts moving off. I fish this way when I've invited my Sunday School class to a fish fry out here."

It would be possible to raise nearly three thousand pounds of catfish per surface acre in a farm pond, but an oxygen-depletion problem could develop if the landowner weren't careful, Armor warned.

"Take them out when they're ¾ of a pound or 1 pound each," he recommended. "You don't need to wait until they get one, two, or three pounds. It's like ripe apples or watermelons. You don't wait until they all are ripe. You pick 'em as fast as they get ripe."

Armor fries, broils, and barbecues catfish, and he also prepares catfish stew, chowder, and fish-head stew. He prefers to cook a fish that weighs from ½ pound to 3 pounds.

He cautions fishermen never to wear a white shirt in a boat because the reflected sunlight will spook the fish. Whoop and holler all you wish, but don't drop anything, like pliers, in the boat, or you'll frighten the fish.

"I've never had a radio playing in my boat," he said. "It may be all right if you have music like Guy Lombardo or Wayne King. But if you get some of these rock groups on the radio, that music would scare the fish, snakes, alligators, and everything else off."

He still wonders about the size of a fish, presumably a cat, that got away in the mouth of Richland Creek near Greensboro years ago.

"We put a new line on an ironwood tree and baited it, and next morning we saw it had been broken," he said. "Next night we used a small trot line and baited it, and the fish broke the line and a small limb.

"The next night we wrapped a piece of copper wire around the tree, and in the morning we saw the hook was straightened in the same spot. The last night we tried baiting a hook again, but didn't get a bite."

Wayne Thomaston cast a small spinning lure on ultra-light tackle to catch this channel catfish in a farm pond.

A Lazy Man's Job

I feel sorry for the folks who have yet to discover one of life's greatest joys—sitting on a river or lake bank and waiting for a bite. Just being there is a heap of fun. Naturally, the bite itself is twice as satisfying as the waiting.

Well, this is true if the right fish comes along and bites, said a north Georgia gentleman, as we chatted in a country store near Flowery Branch, a community just a few minutes' drive from Lake Lanier.

W. D. Swansey, 62, puffed a cigarette and explained, "All I fish for is catfish. Just like to. Fishin' for catfish is a lazy man's job. If a bass hits the minnow, it'll make me about half-mad, and it makes me plumb mad for a bream to bite my hook."

He figures that a bluegill is good for one thing—catfish bait. Swansey shared one of his fishing secrets and told me a bream's head is mighty attractive to a hungry catfish.

A dozen or more medium size minnows swam in a bucket on the rear floorboard of his old car. In the trunk lay nine closed-face reels and rods, which likely have as much mileage as the car.

His biggest blue catfish was a 49-pounder that he pulled out of a private lake.

"You know how big a gallon paint bucket is?" asked the fisherman. "You could'a put a bucket in his mouth. You ain't gonna use too big a bait for them."

A day before we met, Swansey had landed a 17-pound blue catfish in Lake Lanier.

Had he ever seen a catfish break 20-pound test line?

"Not since this time yesterday," said Swansey, glancing at his watch, remembering it was the hour he had planned to bait his hooks.

"One day last year, another fellow and I caught 300 pounds of catfish," he said. "It was the second week of April. We had a slop of 'em. We left Lake Lanier sort of tuckered out."

During the winter, catfish lie in the deep water and eat less than in the warm seasons, but on a sunny day they "come up some" and bite, he says. Little catfish can be taken on hook and line any month, but the bigger catfish bite best in the summer.

Before Lake Lanier was impounded, Swansey fished for cats in the Chattahoochee River.

"We'd get some we couldn't hold, they were so big," he said. "I imagine the biggest in that river would be as long as I am tall. Some might weigh 100 pounds."

He puts a sliding, oval shaped sinker on his line, ties a swivel about eight inches above a No. 2 hook, and rarely uses a cork or wooden bobber.

"When the catfish bites, he just gets the minnow and goes with it," said Swansey. "Hardly ever mouths it. I don't let him run too far if I can keep him from it, because the farther he goes, the more stumps you've got to pull him back by. I try to get him off the bottom quick as I can and not let him go back."

He either lifts the fish out of the water with a landing net or wades into the lake to grab it.

"Sometimes I wade out and put my fingers in his gills and my thumb in the corner of his mouth," said Swansey. "He won't bite your finger off, but he'll make you holler a little bit. As long as he's on that hook swimmin' in the water, he ain't mine. But, when I grab his gills and mouth, he's mine then."

When is the best time to fish for catfish?

"I don't know if the moon makes that much difference," he

said. "They tell me when the signs [of the zodiac] are in the stomach, the fish is full.

"Ain't but one thing I go by. I listen to the weather forecast. When a cold wave is comin' in tomorrow, but it's pretty today, if there's any way I can get to the lake, I'm gonna fish tonight. They will bite before that front comes better than any other time. They can't stand it. We'll put out jugs and bait the hooks with minnows."

The minnows were restless, and Swansey was itching to go fishing. It's not polite to delay a guy who's got business down at the lake.

Watch Your Line "Breathe"

To catch a big catfish in a reservoir or river, a fisherman must learn to recognize his line "breathing."

This slight, rhythmic movement of the line indicates a catfish has swallowed the bait, and he's just lying on the bottom and breathing, says Hoyt McDaniel of Suches, a small community in mountainous Union County in north Georgia.

On a summer afternoon in 1969, McDaniel baited his hook with a large minnow on Lake Nottely in the mountains, and he caught a 51 lb. 15 oz. "yellow catfish" in a battle that lasted one hour and fifteen minutes.

A fisheries biologist who saw a snapshot of the fish said it appeared to be the species called flathead catfish.

McDaniel was standing on the bank that day and fishing with a closed-face spinning reel and 15-pound test line.

"Charles Gordon from Marietta saw me get the big one," said McDaniel. "I showed him how the line was breathing before I tightened the line. The fish had taken the bait and he was lying on the bottom.

"He opens his gills and water squirts out the mouth. The line will wave in perfect rhythm, and when you see that, all you have to do is tighten up a little and the catfish will set the hook himself. He'll start moving when you put a little tension on the line."

His son, Willis B. McDaniel of Buford, Georgia, landed a

42-pound catfish in Lake Nottely. The day before pulling in the 51-pounder, McDaniel caught a 42-pounder and a 21-pound blue cat.

"I don't use a net to land a big catfish," said McDaniel. "All you have to do is run your hand in his mouth and catch down on the ring of his underlip. He will not close his mouth. He'll be perfectly quiet."

Mr. McDaniel, I wouldn't put my hand in a big catfish's mouth for ten crisp ten-dollar bills.

He barbecued his biggest catfish, a chore that required over three hours of cooking.

Baits that he prefers are minnows or big blue worms found in north Georgia. Cats weighing over 15 pounds usually won't take liver, he says, but it's all right for smaller fish in lakes and rivers. It's not uncommon for him to string 30 to 40 catfish in the three- and four-pound class in one day, and he describes Nottely as "one of the best lakes I've ever fished."

"Most people just don't know how to fish for catfish," he added. "They expect the big ones to grab it and run. They throw out their hooks, drag them back in and see there's no bait, and they think a little fish got it. But, big ones do that. He'll swallow it and take off the bait in one minute."

The Suches angler recommended that a fisherman throw out his baited hook, put down the rod and reel, and watch the line. He doesn't ever use a float or bobber.

He explained that the north Georgia blue devil worm, which grows to a length of 8 to 12 inches, is a cross between a Louisiana pink and the black wiggler.

In fishing for cats, McDaniel has his best luck just before sundown, and he likes to fish "when the moon is building up—first quarter or last quarter, or just before it gets full."

"A yellow catfish weighing three pounds on up gives more fight than a bass," he said. "Sometimes he stays on the bottom and lies there like a log. All you have to do is jiggle the line lightly and he will start moving again. At first he will start circling, then you can gradually pull him in."

McDaniel said the 51-pounder from Lake Nottely "was 12 inches across the top of his head, had a girth of at least 36 inches and was approximately 3½ feet long."

XII

Bowfin

His Name Is Mud

In warm, sluggish, shallow streams, lakes, and swamps across the southern states, there lives a fish of great strength and stamina, debatable quality of meat texture and flavor, and a bad reputation.

He has been called numerous names, many of which should not be heard by ladies, even gentlemen for that matter. Some folks in south Georgia and Florida call him the mudfish; in the Okefenokee Swamp he is often called a cypress trout, and in some states he is the black fish or grinnel.

Biologists and record-keepers speak of him as the bowfin. You might even refer to the rugged critter as a living fossil, because he probably was swimming in southern waters about the time Adam and Eve stumbled upon an apple and a snake in the Garden of Eden.

The bowfin has a long dorsal fin, an olive or gray back and sides, and light colored belly, with sharp teeth, small scales, and a tough skin. The male bowfin has an orange and yellow-rimmed spot on its tail, but the female doesn't have such a rim, and the spot is not present in all fish.

An air sac or bladder provides the bowfin with a primitive sort of auxiliary respiratory system. I have watched them rise to the surface as if they are gulping air on a hot summer day, and they can remain alive on the bottom of a boat or on a dew-covered bank a surprising length of time.

During my youth in Waycross, Georgia, I caught hundreds of bowfin—we called them mudfish—on shiny or brightly-colored, shallow-running plugs, silver spoons, and flashy spinning lures in the Okefenokee Swamp.

They would chomp down so hard on a wooden plug that teeth marks were left in the body, and treble hooks frequently were straightened by the fish's brute strength on a run.

The bowfin were crazy about the Johnson spoon and pork rind, the shallow running Hawaiian Wiggler with yellow or red-and-white skirt, the Scrambled Egg (Pflueger Pal-O-Mine in scrambled red, orange, and yellow finish), and the Pflueger Fluted Spoon that had a red and silver blade and a red, yellow, and white skirt. I remember catching dozens on a rainbow-colored Heddon Vamp and the Creek Chub Darter in a silver-flash finish.

When the black bass wouldn't bite in the summer when the water was so warm, my fishing partner and I got relief from the boredom by trolling baits for the mudfish in Billy's Lake and the Suwannee Canal in the Okefenokee. Once I took my nephews, Randy and Darrell Saltsgaver of Winter Park, Florida, fishing in Billy's Lake, and Randy pulled a mudfish to the side of the boat that must have weighed close to 13 pounds. I was sort of happy when his line broke, because a mudfish with a treble hook-lined plug in its jaws, thrashing around in a boat, can be a dangerous threat to a fellow's ankles, legs, and hands.

Record-Breaking Living Fossil

Robert L. Harmon, 54, a Florence, South Carolina, fiber plant worker, went fishing for largemouth bass on January 29, 1980, in 200-acre Forest Lake, a short distance from his home. He didn't have the good fortune to catch a humongous bass, but he pulled out a critter that lacked only 13 ounces of exceeding the weight of that 22 lb. 4 oz. record largemouth.

Harmon saw to his dismay that it was a lowly bowfin. The living fossil weighed 21 lb. 8 oz., and was 36 inches long.

He was notified later in the year that this fish was declared by the National Fresh Water Fishing Hall of Fame in Hayward, Wisconsin, to be a world record bowfin. Harmon laughed and told me, "Some of my friends were jealous, and some were happy. Yes, some envied it."

The giant bowfin was hooked about eleven o'clock that morning while Harmon was trolling for bass in the lake, which is divided by a bridge and road.

"I was fishing with a brand new plug that day," he said. "It was a rainbow-colored Rebel. It sure was cold on the lake. I was trolling in water about eight feet deep, and thought I had hooked a little bass.

"I had been catching bass. The mudfish got halfway to my boat, and he must have figured something was wrong, and he began to raise sand. He went the other way, and all I could do was hang on."

He was fishing with an Ambassadeur baitcasting reel, a Lew Childre graphite rod, and 20-pound test monofilament line.

"You know, you don't bring a mudfish in quickly," said Harmon. "He will fight you every step of the way. He came up and rolled. He won't walk on his tail like a bass. In about ten minutes, I had him next to the boat. Believe it or not, I had him in the net three times, and every time I'd go to pick him up, he'd slide out."

The 21½-pound bowfin "like to have tore up my net" before it finally was dropped into the boat. Harmon carefully removed a treble hook embedded in the side of the fish's mouth.

He decided that he would retire the new plug and let it hang from the jaw of the bowfin after a taxidermist prepared it for display on a wall in his home.

"I believe the mudfish is stronger than a bass," he said. "The mudfish might be our next sport fish. I've been talking to a South Carolina wildlife man about it."

His biggest bowfin in past years was a 14-pounder, and he also has taken a 12-pounder. His biggest black bass ever was a 9 lb. 8 oz. lunker that struck a Hula Popper.

"I love to use those topwater plugs," said Harmon. "There's something exciting when the water explodes."

The previous world record bowfin also was taken in South Carolina waters. M. R. Webster pulled a 19 lb. 12 oz. bowfin out of Lake Marion in the Santee-Cooper system on November 5, 1972. Georgia's state record bowfin weighed 16 pounds and was caught in the Okefenokee Swamp near Stephen Foster State Park by Charles O. Conley on May 25, 1976.

An Unwanted Monster

One of my fishing friends, Jerry Rogers, a Fulton County, Georgia, fireman, tangled with the biggest bowfin ever boated in Georgia, but he was quite reluctant to describe the experience. Jerry is a dyed-in-the-wool bass fisherman, so you understand his reaction.

While casting on Georgia's Bartletts Ferry, he spotted a log lying in shallow, stained water next to the bank and felt it might be appealing to a bass waiting to ambush a minnow.

Jerry, who counts bass, not sheep, when he's trying to fall asleep, said, "I saw that log and told my fishin' partner, 'I'll bet there's a hawg lyin' beside that thing.' "

He cast a chartreuse-and-black spinnerbait with copper blades to the bank and pulled it along the side of the log.

"The fish jumped on that spinnerbait and I popped the hook to him," said Jerry, "and you never saw such a big black thing thrashing around."

Fearing the fish would cut his line on the log and snags, Jerry decided he would have to go for broke and try to horse him in. He turned to his fishing partner and advised him to get ready.

"There ain't hardly any way I can get that joker out unless I reel like there's no tomorrow," Jerry yelled. "In that mess of stumps, I've got just one shot. I'll reel like crazy and you grab the net."

The huge fish broke water, but neither angler got a good look at its head or tail, only glimpsing a big girth and dark back through the spray. In a moment, half of the fish was in the net, its tail swinging in the air like a sledge hammer. Both men couldn't believe their eyes.

Jerry had put in the boat a 16 lb. 7 oz. bowfin, which would have topped the state record of 16 pounds.

"That crazy fish like to have torn the bottom out of my bass boat," said Jerry. "I ran to the bow, and my partner to the stern. We let the bowfin have the center of the boat. That crazy fish knocked over two tackle boxes, spilling plugs everywhere, and broke the handle of my spinning rod. I got a stick and tried to kill him, but it just made him mad every time I hit him."

The spinnerbait was practically destroyed by the powerful jaws and sharp teeth of the bowfin; the trailer hook was straightened, and the lure's steel arms that resemble an open safety pin were bent out of shape.

"I gave the fish to two men who had caught several small catfish off a dock," said Jerry. "The bowfin was thrashing around like something wild, and this joker jumped on his back and tried to kill him.

"He put him on a rope stringer, and the bowfin chewed it in two. Finally he put the bowfin in a five-gallon bucket, with the tail hanging out. While they were tussling with the bowfin, some of the little catfish jumped back in the lake."

Jerry, who wouldn't have given 50 cents for the big fish, was sorry that his spinnerbait was torn up. However, he confessed, "That monster was the strongest thing I've ever hooked. Oh, if only it'd been a bass. I just knew I'd hooked the biggest bass in Bartletts Ferry."

XIII
Dabbling—"Jigger-Fishing"

For Explosive Strikes

Some folks call it "dabbling." Many others prefer the name passed down by their grandfathers—"jigger-fishing." The very tiring but highly productive method of fishing for black bass on the surface with a long, strong cane pole and a homemade lure was being used more than two hundred years ago on south Georgia rivers. A number of southern fishermen still are hooking lunkers on jigger poles today.

The famed naturalist William Bartram, who traveled through Georgia and Florida in the early 1770s, watched two men fishing in a canoe with a 10- to 12-foot pole, 20 inches of line, and three big hooks. They had made a bob by covering the hooks with hair from a deer's tail, pieces of a red garter, and colored feathers that formed a tassel almost as large as a man's fist.

One of the men paddled quietly, keeping the canoe parallel to the bank and close enough for the angler to reach the edge of weeds with the pole.

Bartram wrote, "He now ingeniously swings the bob backwards and forwards, just above the surface, and sometimes tips the water with it; when the unfortunate cheated trout (largemouth bass) instantly springs from under the weeds and seizes the supposed prey.

"Thus he is caught without a possibility of escape unless he breaks the hooks, line, or rod, which he, however, sometimes does by dint of strength. But, to prevent this, the fisherman used to the sport is careful not to raise the reed suddenly up, but jerks it instantly backwards, then steadily drags the sturdy reluctant fish to the side of the canoe, and, with a sudden upright jerk, brings him into it."

Jigger-fishing requires a strong back, strong arms, and a good friend who will paddle the boat very quietly, keeping you close enough to the bank to reach out and drop the lure beside stumps, logs, trees, and grass.

Tie some 40- to 100-pound test braided line two joints back from the end of a 12- to 16-foot fiberglass or cane pole, and tie it again on the tip, leaving 6 to 24 inches of line to work the bait.

Revenal Winge of Waycross, Georgia, who left his heart on the beautiful Altamaha River when he first tangled with huge bass over 15 years ago, says the oldtimers still like to cut a lure in the shape of a lizard from the tongue of a boot and jig it next to the banks. He favors surface plugs with spluttering propellers on the front and back to create a racket.

"Some of us use only six inches of line and pull an old Buel spinner or Marathon Husky Hawk across the top of the water," he said. "It's not as much work as jigging a lure up and down.

"Jigger-fishing attracts a lot of big bass, some up to eight or ten pounds, and you catch a world of small bass with this commotion. When a bass strikes, the sound of the big splash can be heard a long way up and down the river. The jigger pole is almost snatched out of your hands."

After the explosive strike, the fisherman quickly pulls the pole toward him, rather than upward, to set the hook, and he continues this movement until the fish is within reach of the landing net.

"You run the lure over the surface close to the banks and beside the stumps and logs and grass," said Winge. "You cover a lot more water this way than in baitcasting. When a bass is lying under there watching the surface action, he sometimes hits the lure on an impulse. He may be hungry, or you may just make him mad.

"You won't catch a bass every time one jumps on your lure. He sometimes strikes short. Jigger-fishing is best in the fall and spring, but you can land some big ones in the winter when the water is cold and the fish aren't as active."

Fishermen using jigger poles have found productive some surface plugs with propellers on the front and back, such as the Devil's Horse, Nip-i-diddee, and Dying Flutter. Another good bait on the rivers is a black plastic lizard, which can be jigged up and down near the banks.

If you like to make your own lures, a good jigger-fishing bait can be fashioned from a large treble hook with feathers or bucktail and a big spinner blade. Some of the oldtimers like to cut pieces of pork rind or a strip of flannel to add to the action. Then, make as much commotion as possible and hang on.

While his partner paddles the boat, the fisherman works his bait in a figure-eight pattern, constantly bumping the end of the pole with his hand. The bait should flop up and down on the water. As one angler observed, "It's a bone-killing job, and they usually have to swap ends of the boat every half hour because it's so tiring."

This method of fishing usually is most effective early in the morning and late in the afternoon. Fishing is usually better when rains have stained the rivers.

When Lake Seminole was filled in the late 1950s, fishermen used to put a big gob of pond worms on treble hooks and ease along the banks and drop the bait beside a stump. After the bait reached the bottom, the angler lifted it up and down, and soon it was struck by a big bass, a channel catfish, or a bowfin.

* * *

Barney Cone, a retired law enforcement officer for the U.S. Department of the Interior, said that jigger-fishing has been popular down on the Suwannee River and in the Okefenokee Swamp for 75 years, perhaps longer.

When Cone was a kid in Fargo, Georgia, fishermen made

lures by cutting the tongue out of a shoe or boot, shaping it like a lizard, and lining it with hooks. The lure was worked in a figure-eight pattern or S-shaped path across the surface of the water.

Largemouth bass (many swamp fishermen still call them "trout," as did their grandfathers and great-grandfathers) with mouths larger than one-pound coffee cans, tried to destroy the thing and made anglers' hearts flutter in excitement.

"I make my own bait," said Cone, who used to patrol the Okefenokee and track down poachers and moonshiners. "It's just a wad of feathers and two sets of treble hooks. I usually use white feathers, but I don't think it makes much difference. I think what the fish strikes at is the noise and action the bait is making on top of the water."

In Fargo, the temperature drops to the freezing mark only an average of 19 days during the year, so jigger-pole fishing can be done virtually every month.

"You just keep the bait on the surface," said Cone. "Your line is 3½ to 4 inches long. I make a homemade line that would hold a six- or seven-foot alligator, so I'm not scared of a fish breaking it. It's probably 80- to 100-pound test.

"It's done in a figure-eight motion. I guess that's what you call it. It's a steady beat on the water, like a frog jumpin', flip, flip, flip, around the edges, stumps, and logs."

His biggest bass taken on a jigger pole have ranged from 10 to 12 pounds. Barney's largest bass, however, weighed 13 lb. 9 oz., and swallowed a plastic worm with little propeller and beads.

When is the best time to jigger-fish for bass?

"I think it depends on the moon," said Cone. "I like to fish with the moon up and the moon down. Sometimes I fish in the Suwannee River on moonlight nights.

"Usually fishing is good all night on a full moon or two or three days before and after a full moon. A new moon is a little too dark. Jigger-fishing definitely is better at night and with the moonlight. You can run the bait in weeds and grass.

"You can hold it up between you and the moon and see if it has grass or weeds on it. Fish won't bite nothin' with grass on it."

The Fargo fisherman has pulled 10- to 15-pound bowfin out of the Suwannee River and Okefenokee with jigger poles. The chain pickerel, or jackfish, also attack the feathered bait, but Barney wishes they would ignore it. A jackfish's razor-sharp teeth can rip a good lure to smithereens.

"Sometimes a fish breaks your pole," he said. "And sometimes you break it yourself trying to pick him up too quick. The fish are still green when you get them in the boat.

"I have missed a whole lots of strikes, but I don't think the fish was really tryin' to catch it. He was just fightin' at it, not wantin' to catch anything to eat but just to let you know he was there."

XIV

Fish Tales— Some Tall, Some True

Hubert Greene thanked his little pal, Fudgey the duck, for pointing to the location of this huge largemouth bass in a Florida lake. Greene then proceeded to offer the fish a plastic worm, and it struck the artificial bait—much to Fudgey's delight.

Fudgey Finds the Big'uns

A dog might be man's best friend, but a duck can be a guy's best fishing partner, a North Carolina bass fisherman has convinced me.

Hubert Greene, operator of a marine dealership on Lake Lure near Spindale, North Carolina, told me that he had caught a number of trophy-size largemouth bass that he probably wouldn't have been able to locate if his extraordinary pet duck had not been present to go on point—sort of like a trained pointer does when he finds a covey of quail.

This may sound like a quacky fish yarn, but it's true, and Fudgey's amazing bass-finding performances have been witnessed by many of Hubert's fishing companions.

One summer morning Hubert decided to go bass fishing on Lake Lure, and the pet mallard duck waddled along just for the ride. Little did he dream that his friendly passenger could be of any value in angling.

As Hubert slowly eased along the bank with a bow-mounted electric motor on his bass boat, Fudgey the duck suddenly concluded that two could fish better than one. The young duck swam near a bush, stopped and stuck his neck out as far as it could reach, as if he were on point.

Greene jokingly told his fishing partner in the stern of the boat, "I believe a bass is over there."

He cast a soft plastic worm close to the bush, and the fake

wiggler was seized by a four-pound black bass. Greene removed the hook from the fish's jaw, thinking it was an accident the way Fudgey had pointed.

Fudgey, however, repeated his bass-pointing act several more times, convincing Greene this was no mere series of coincidences.

In a North Carolina mountain lake, Fudgey had a close call that nearly scared the feathers off his back.

Hubert's wife, Rose, who enjoys her role as Fudgey's "mother," said, "Hubert wondered what Fudgey would do if he saw a really big bass. Well, when they were fishing one day Fudgey swam to a fallen tree and suddenly yelled and flapped his wings—scared half to death, and hurried back to the boat. Hubert cast a spinnerbait over there and hooked a nine-pound largemouth bass."

Before the last rays of sunshine touched the lake that day, the talented mallard duck pointed again, and Greene cast an artificial lure into the area and caught a ten-pound bass.

Hubert and Rose told me that the duck was about three days old, lost and very frightened when their son, Todd, 15, found him one day in July near their boat dock on Lake Lure.

She said, "The duck was yellow with brown streaks, striped-like, and Todd laughed and said, 'He looks like fudge rippled ice cream.' So, we named him Fudgey. We hunted his mother for several days, and by the time we found her, she didn't recognize her baby duck, and we carried Fudgey back home and took care of him."

The little duck was taught to swim by its unfeathered, wingless "parents."

"Fudgey was scared and would practically walk on top of the water," said Rose. "Finally mama and daddy put on their bathing suits and gave him swimming lessons. We waved our arms like wings, and he started imitating us and began swimming. Later, Hubert would dive, duck under and got Fudgey to diving, too."

Next Hubert started taking the pet duck for boat rides,

allowing Fudgey to swim beside the bass boat while he was casting. Fudgey did some fishing, too, grabbing minnows in shallow water near the bank.

That first year Fudgey accompanied the Greenes to their marine dealership, and each night he slept on a pallet beside their bed in the lakeside home. The little duck wasn't housebroken—"How do you housebreak a duck?" So Rose served him an early supper and let him go for a walk in the evening. Fudgey curled up in his master's lap on the sofa in front of the television set and appeared to enjoy the outdoor shows much more than the situation comedies and the cops-and-robbers dramas.

Fudgey is quite fond of ripe tomatoes, and at breakfast he is happy to see the family serve a brand of cereal that contains raisins.

In the fishing boat, Fudgey sometimes fetches the plastic worms that Hubert wants to cast for bass. The reds and purples give him a fit, but blues and blacks are easier for him to find. Hubert points to the trays in his tackle box so that Fudgey will pick up the right color.

Fudgey seems to perform best in a lake that is crystal clear, spotting fish not only in shallow areas close to the banks but also in water that is even 10 to 15 feet deep.

Fudgey once surprised his master by giving him an unusual, awfully big Christmas present, and although the delivery was a day late, Hubert didn't seem to mind.

The Greenes had decided to take Fudgey with them to Florida's Lake Okeechobee during the Christmas holidays. On December 26, they passed through Kissimmee to see Lake Toho where Hubert planned to compete in a bass fishing tournament the following month.

"It was already late evening, but Hubert decided to go out for about an hour before proceeding on to Okeechobee," said Rose, who, though tired, picked up Fudgey and her camera and went along for the ride.

"Fudgey was fascinated with all the gulls and cranes. He

wanted to go swimming, but we were afraid of the alligators, so we insisted he stay in the boat. We did allow him up on the casting platform in front of the bass boat with Hubert. We hadn't been out 15 minutes when Fudgey went on point."

On more than 25 fishing trips with the duck, Hubert had learned that when Fudgey stuck his neck out and pointed toward a tree, stump, or submerged brush, it would be wise to cast a lure into the spot. But, in this instance, Hubert already had fished the shallow grass bed at which Fudgey continued to point.

Rose said, "Come on. You owe Fudgey one more time."

Hubert cast a black Jelly Worm into the area, but failed to get a strike. His wife turned to the pet duck and said, "Come back here with me, little fellow. Your efforts aren't appreciated today." She offered the duck a tomato "to make him feel loved and consoled."

The boat was almost out of casting range of the grass bed, when Hubert decided it might be wise to make another cast, just in case Fudgey really had seen a fish.

A 12-pound largemouth bass struck the soft plastic worm, and Hubert set the hook. Within a few minutes, he was gripping the lower jaw of the biggest bass that he has caught since Fudgey began pointing fish for him.

In the previous summer and fall, Fudgey's best points had enabled his master to catch a number of lunkers in the 7- to 11-pound class.

Hubert and Rose were very proud of Fudgey's performance on the big Florida lake. She told her husband, "You'd never have looked back if it hadn't been for Fudgey."

They drove to a bait shop and rewarded Fudgey with a dozen delicious minnows.

Leroy—A Fighter and Lover

Each year thousands of tourists visit Tom Mann's Fish World, located several miles north of Eufaula, Alabama, to observe with fascination the many species of freshwater pan fish and game fish swimming in aquariums designed to resemble natural fish habitats.

They pause outside to admire the handsome marble sculpture of a largemouth bass mounted on a grave marker bearing this inscription: "Most bass are just fish, but Leroy Brown was something special."

Leroy Brown, who was despised by other male bass, but loved dearly by every female bass in a 38,000-gallon aquarium, was undoubtedly the most unforgettable largemouth bass ever hooked by Tom Mann, a fishing lure manufacturer and bass tournament champion.

A year before Leroy died, I visited Fish World, and Mann described the remarkable habits, behavior, and lifestyle of the fish, already a legend in his own time.

"Leroy is a fighter, and he's a great lover," said Mann. "He can get mighty jealous and mean if somebody messes around with his girlfriend. I don't know how many thousands of children Leroy is claiming these days. When I caught Leroy, he weighed one pound. I put him in the aquarium and noticed him standing out. He was streamlined and had a sharper nose, and his eyes were farther back on his head."

Quite a scrapper, Leroy kept other bass out of his jealously guarded territory in the aquarium that Mann viewed from a large window in his office. Later he moved Leroy to the 38,000-gallon aquarium at the tourist attraction.

Mann taught Leroy to jump through a hoop to grab a minnow, and soon the fish learned to rise to the surface and grab a minnow out of his hand.

When Mann discovered that Leroy had died one morning in late summer, 1980, he described the loss as being as great, perhaps worse, than seeing one's favorite bird dog die.

Mann said Leroy had died "of exhaustion and over-exertion" shortly after his seventh birthday, an age he called equivalent to 70 years in a human's life.

Leroy probably never completely recovered from the death two years earlier of his beloved Big Bertha, a largemouth bass weighing ten pounds, the favorite of his eight "wives."

Leroy's body was placed in a freezer, and the lure designer set out to make arrangements for an elaborate bass funeral. It was to be held several months later on March 18, 1981, on Lake Walter F. George, after the weigh-in of fish on the opening day of a Bass Anglers Sportsman Society fishing tournament.

On that windy, rainy, cool afternoon, more than six hundred persons from across the nation—including bass tournament contestants, reporters, photographers, and television newsmen and crews—assembled in the auditorium of an Alabama state resort park to pay tribute to a fish that was eulogized as "something special."

Ray Scott of Montgomery, president of 380,000-member Bass Anglers Sportsman Society, stood in a red, handsomely-equipped bass boat and recalled that the "unique, intelligent" bass "took command of the aquarium from the moment he was introduced" six years before, after Mann caught him in Lake George, and that "wherever he swam, the females followed Leroy with their eyes."

Scott noted that each time Mann designed a new fishing lure, he "consulted Leroy," but the wary fish never was hooked again, although he curiously followed each invention around the aquarium. Sometimes Mann dropped a lure with hooks into Leroy's spawning nest, but the cautious fish guarding the eggs would gently pick up the artificial bait without touching the hook points and drop it several feet away.

The B.A.S.S. president said he was thankful God created the great game fish, the largemouth bass, and he declared that Leroy was a very worthy representative of the species. He expressed appreciation that we can enjoy bass fishing in the greatest nation on earth.

Scott removed his western hat when a baby cried in the crowd, then held the hat over his heart and gazed solemnly at Leroy Brown, who was lying in a satin-lined tackle box converted into a casket.

He read a telegram from Alabama Governor Fob James, who said Leroy "was known and loved by many, and I know he will certainly be missed." The governor proclaimed an official day of mourning for Leroy in the state of Alabama.

Country singer Jerry Reed wired this message: "Tom, our heartfelt sympathy goes out to you and one of the greatest fighters of all time, Leroy Brown. May he rest in peace in that great bass world in the sky."

Homer Circle of *Sports Afield* magazine said in a telegram, "Somehow ol' Leroy represents that mystical bond between all dedicated bass fishermen and the bass. It's a kinship only a bassin' man can understand, and I feel privileged to have known your departed buddy who taught you there is much to admire in all bass. From now on, as I release each bass I catch, if you listen closely you'll hear Uncle Homer murmur, 'There's one for ol' Leroy.'"

Pallbearers placed strawberry-flavored Jelly Worms, the bait Mann had used to fool Leroy in Lake George, on the body of the celebrated bass before burial at the foot of the marble sculpture. The pallbearers included bass tournament champions Roland Martin, Paul Chamblee, Randy Fite, Jimmy Houston, John Powell, Forrest Wood, Rayo Breckenridge, Hank Parker, Bo Dowden, and Bobby Murray.

Then hundreds of persons clapped in time with the beat of the music as Billy Wilbourne sang "Bad, Bad Leroy Brown," the Jim Croce song that inspired Mann to name his "bad, bad bass."

Burial of the famed fish was postponed because of rain. The next morning Fish World workers discovered that the remains of the 6 lb. 2 oz. Leroy Brown and the tackle-box coffin had been taken from a freezer in the building.

"The back door was broken open," said Mann, "and Leroy was gone. I couldn't believe it. Frozen shad and minnows we feed the fish in aquariums had been thrown onto the floor. It was a mess. They got 40 bags of Jelly Worms, each containing 100 worms, all eight inches long."

Mann said a ransom note scrawled in pencil on a cardboard box said, "We have Leroy Brown, and we are asking 1½ miles of Jelly Worms. More to come."

The burglar removed a mounted largemouth bass from a wall in Mann's bass tournament trophy display section and threw it into the muddy hole where Leroy was to have been buried.

Mann, who offered a $10,000 reward for information leading to arrest and conviction of the burglar, had expected a prank and feared someone would try to dig up the fish.

A policeman said, "One fish looks like another. You couldn't tell him (Leroy) from another fish."

But, I think Mann would recognize bad, old Leroy Brown, his favorite lure consultant.

Mann told me he showed his wife, Ann, the marble headstone and sculpture of Leroy several weeks before the funeral.

"She asked, 'What's the other grave site for?' " said Mann, "and, I said, 'Honey, that one's for you.' She said, 'I hope you spend as much for mine as you spent for his.' And, I said, 'You'd better believe I will.' "

Bulger—An Angling Legend

If Bulger could talk, he'd tell some downright hair-raising tales of his big battles with the giants. If the little guy could write, he surely would produce a best-seller with his blood-curdling descriptions of the dozens of times that he was nearly skinned alive.

Bulger, acting alone on extremely dangerous missions in no-man's territory, truly has become a legend in his own time in Georgia.

When fishermen participate in bull sessions about the best baits to use, Bulger easily emerges as the bravest of the brave—especially if his master is present.

Bulger is an 8½-inch ground puppy, or hellbender, an aquatic salamander, that hibernates each winter in a box next to the furnace in the home of his master, George Wilson of Thomaston, Georgia.

George insists that, with the help of Bulger as the irresistible bait, he has caught "around eight hundred pounds" of largemouth bass in farm ponds and Georgia's Flint River since 1970. The biggest bass that has grabbed little Bulger so far was a 14 lb. 8 oz. lunker that tried to eat its last supper in a pond near tiny Williamson, Georgia.

Some fishermen may be tempted to accuse me of confusing truth and fantasy, but old George is mighty proud of his pet hellbender, and he wanted me to know of Bulger's bassin' record. You decide for yourself whether ol' Bulger is the real thing or an amusing myth.

George, who is regarded by folks in Thomaston as a good ol' boy and who, in fact, is a successful bass fisherman, advised me never to bet that Bulger won't pop to the surface and shake his head after failing to find a bass at home in "hawg holes."

George's association with Bulger began in 1970, when he stopped at a bait shop and bought some lizards that had been found in Yellow Jacket Creek. One of them was special.

"He was rare because he was brown with yellow spots, not like the other black-and-white salamanders," said George. "He was three inches long."

The Georgia fisherman decided to name him after his pet bulldog.

"I credit his longevity to his size," said George. "The fish strike, and when I set the hook and they jump, they sling him up the line and I reel him on in. The fool hangs onto the cork most of the time when the hook is in the fish's jaw. I usually fish Bulger three feet deep with a cork and two pieces of lead 18 inches above him."

On several occasions, friends of George Wilson have lost bets that the brave hellbender wouldn't surface and shake his head to indicate the fish weren't home.

"By nature he is a floater and comes up," said George. "The two pieces of lead make him sink to the bottom, but he then paddles back to the top, swimming and shaking his head. I give him a minute or two. He comes up for a gulp of air. Then I say, 'Is a bass in there, Bulger?' If a bass is in the pothole, he, of course, gets him. When the cork goes under, the bass has picked him up. I don't give him time to swallow Bulger."

Yearling bass skin or bruise Bulger more than the bigger fish, says George, who claims that he carries little strips of Band Aid in case there's a medical emergency.

"If he gets skinned up bad, it takes five or six days to heal," said George, still in a serious tone. "The hook? I put it in the lower lip, and that heals in a day or two."

If George fails to set the hook in a bass that picked up the bait, Bulger becomes angry and nibbles at his finger.

"Bulger is bedded down hibernating in a box with clay and moss next to my furnace in the basement every winter," said George. "He starts hibernating the second week of December. I'll hear him scratching on the furnace around the first of March to let me know he wants to go fishing. He is getting a little old now. He used to go for three or four hours in the river, but I can't hold him down over two hours now."

George claims that Bulger missed the 1972 fishing season because he developed a serious case of the mumps. He would have us believe that he lets Bulger go out for stud fees at bait shops. "I get the pick of the litter."

George feared that Bulger was lost one day in the spring when he and friends camped and fished in the Flint River.

"Old Bulger was feeling his oats, and he got out of the box one night," said George. "I thought he was a goner. On the third day, he returned to our camp tired but grinning from ear to ear."

If you buy some hellbenders for fish bait this spring and notice that one is brown with yellow spots, it might be one of Bulger's hundreds of children. Even if it is only half as talented as Bulger in bass fishing, you've got a sho' nuff lunker hunter, according to George.

Hey! Stop That Bird!

Don't suggest to Tommy Meeks of Forest Park, Georgia, that a bird in the hand is worth two in the bush. He already has learned the hard way. Laughing, although it must have hurt, he said the bird that he had in mind was worth about $100.

On Tommy's trip with several friends to fish for largemouth bass in Florida's Orange Lake in early March, 1980, the weather was fit for polar bears, and his strange fishing experience was strictly for the birds.

"It was sleeting, the wind was blowing 18 to 20 miles an hour, and it was foggy," said Tommy. "Not what you'd call a perfect day for bass fishing. Jimmy Palmer had told me big bass struck those large shiners, but he didn't inform me about the big birds."

The Georgian baited his hook with a shiner that weighed as much as a hand-size bluegill and cast his bait to the edge of some lily pads in Orange Lake. Soaking wet and feeling quite miserable, Tommy put down his new baitcasting reel and brand-new graphite rod, and he shivered as sleet pelted him and his partner in the bass boat.

"I looked around at our friends' boat, and when I looked back, a large hawk was coming in about ten feet off the water," he said, "with claws ready to grab my shiner on the surface."

He reached for his rod and reel, but the hungry hawk beat him to the draw.

"The bird grabbed the shiner and flew off, and jerked my rod and reel out of the boat," said Tommy. "I was stunned and couldn't believe it. I told Mr. Palmer, Jimmy's daddy, 'That hawk got my rod and reel.'

"At first the rod sank, and the hawk flew on, and my fishing rod jumped out of that water like a big, old bass trying to spit out a plastic worm."

Tommy was incredulous as he stared at the hawk, flapping its wings with 30 or more feet of monofilament line leading straight down from its talons to the fishing rod that was being hauled in a vertical position in the air.

The rod handle and reel dipped into the water and skipped across the surface, and rose about six feet into the air several times, while the tiring hawk flew toward shore to enjoy a fish lunch.

"The hawk had a 200-yard head start on me," said Tommy, "and, I told Mr. [Arvel] Palmer, 'I'm going after that rod and reel.' I pulled up the anchor and started my 85 hp outboard motor.

"I could see I was gaining on the bird. We heard the rod and reel going through the water and lily pads. We went through the lily pads wide open, and I said, 'No, no, don't break the line.' "

Each time the fishing rod fell into the water and lily pads, the big bird flapped its strong wings even harder, eventually stripping almost 50 yards off the reel's spool against the drag's pressure.

"I caught up with the rod and was fixing to grab it," said Tommy, "and the hawk went to the left, and the rod slammed against my boat and went under. The bird was tired. The rod was dragged in the lily pads again, and the line broke.

"The bird got higher and higher, and the last thing I saw was that red-and-white cork near the end of that line in the air under him. We went in the lily pads but couldn't find my rod and reel in five to eight feet of water. If I'd seen it, I'd have taken a dip. That rod and reel were my favorites. I had a sick feeling in my stomach."

Tommy considered reporting the "theft" to his insurance agent, but he suspected the story wouldn't be believed.

XV

Illustrations

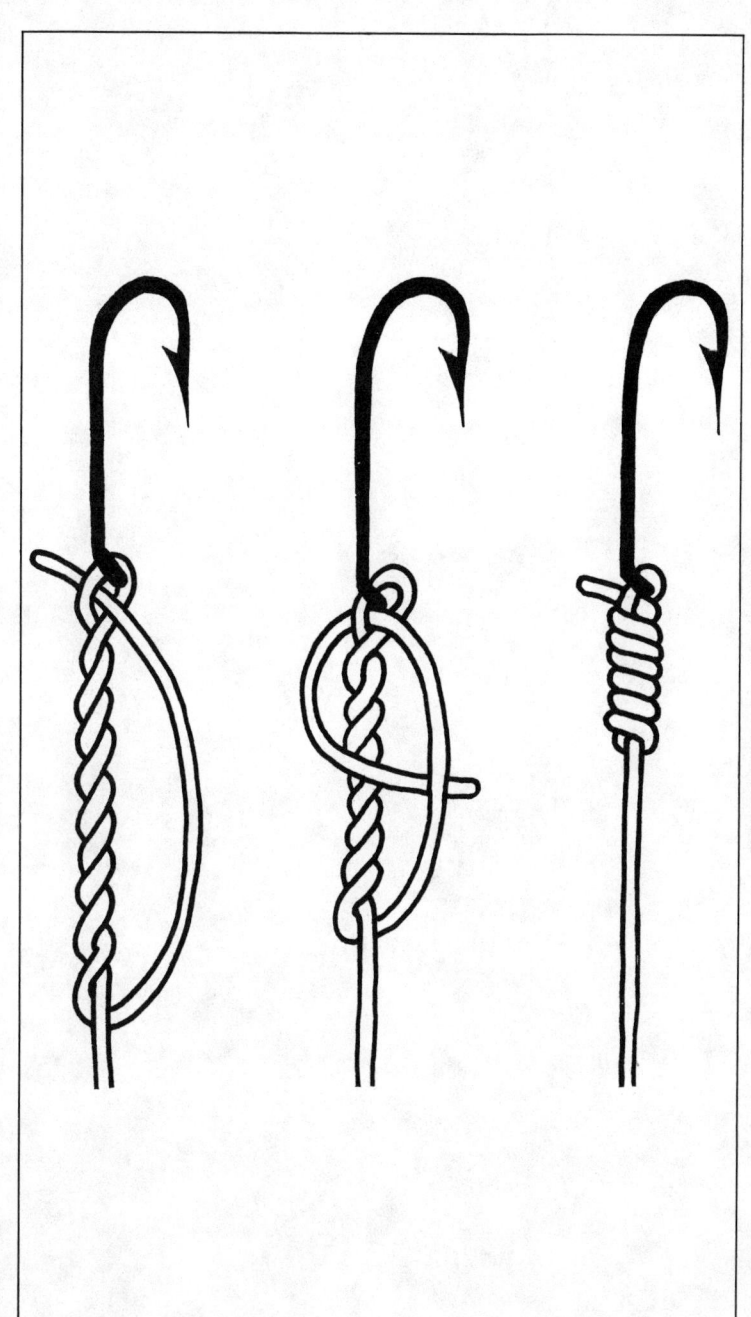

IMPROVED CLINCH KNOT

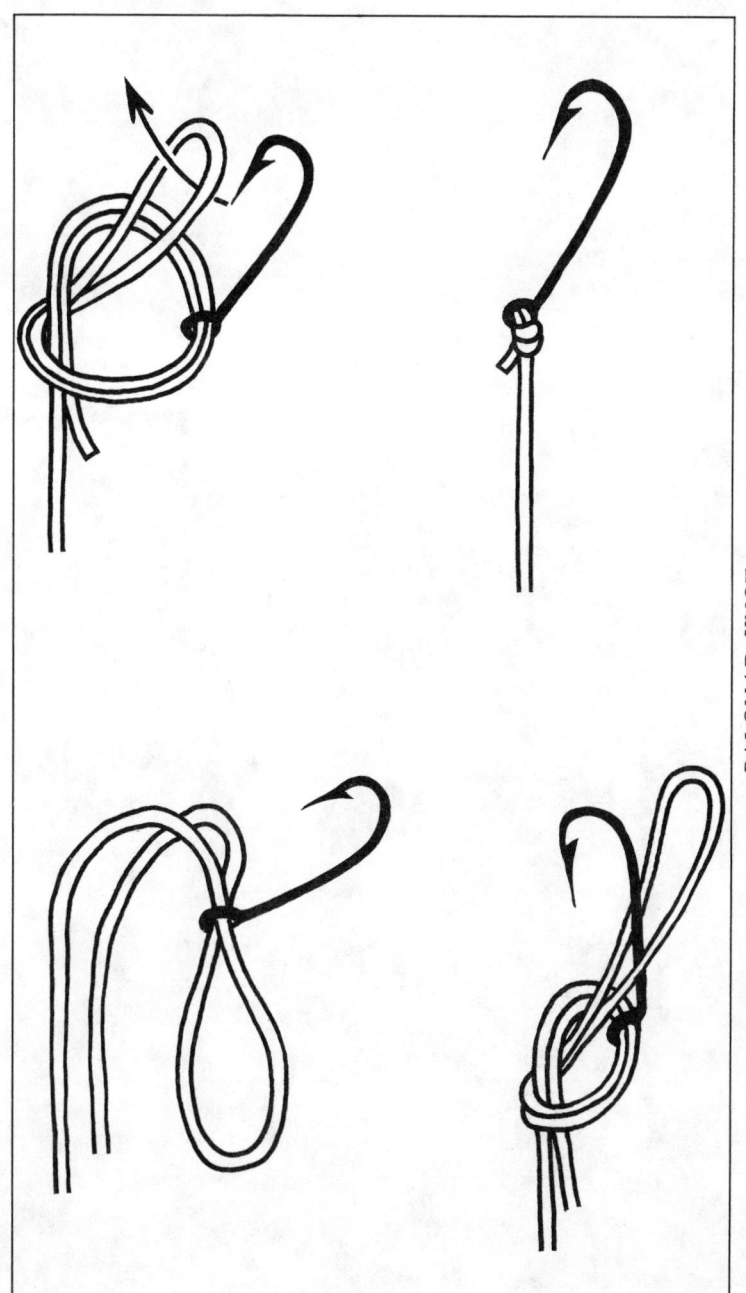

PALOMAR KNOT

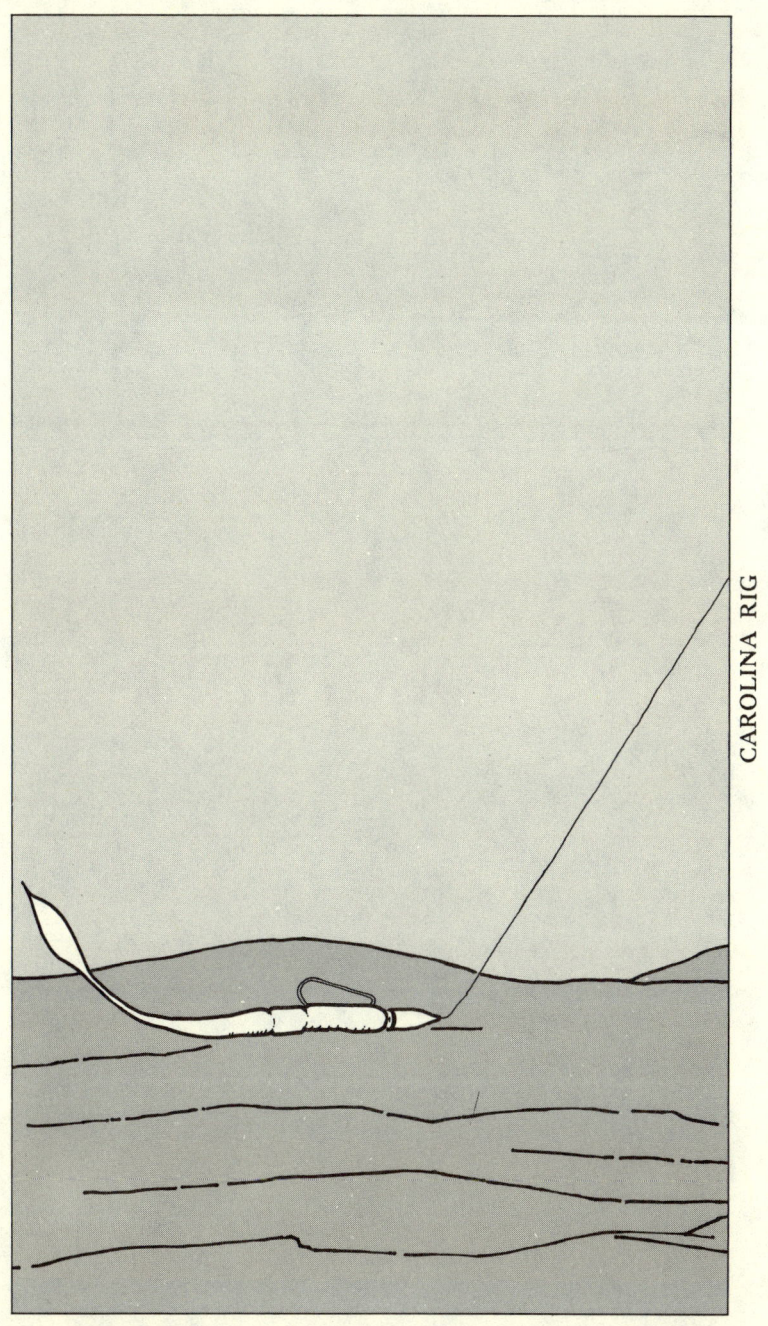

TEXAS RIG